ACOUSTIC GUITAR GUIDES

CLASSICAL GUITAR
ANSWER BOOK
By SHARON ISBIN

STRING LETTER PUBLISHING

Publisher: David A. Lusterman
Editorial Director: Jeffrey Pepper Rodgers
Editor: Simone Solondz
Cover Designer: Elena Tapiero Brown
Interior Designer: Ellen Toomey
Production Manager: Christi Payne

Music Engraving: Janet Smith
Cover photo: Stewart O'Shields

© 1994, 1999 Sharon Isbin
ISBN 1-890490-08-3

Printed in the United States of America.

STRING LETTER PUBLISHING

Contents

Foreword by Jeffrey Pepper Rodgers   5

Introduction by Sharon Isbin   7

Equipment   9

   Auditioning a Guitar   9

   Choosing the Right Scale Length   10

   Cedar vs. Spruce Tops   11

   Instrument Care and Repair   11

   Locating Rattles   13

   Testing Strings   14

   Changing Strings   14

   Footstools   15

   Amplification Setups   16

   Traveling with a Guitar   18

Starters   19

   Tuning Up   19

   Finding a Comfortable Playing Position   20

   Playing Lefty   21

   Lessons for Children   21

   Single Notes vs. Chords for Beginners   21

   Finding the Right Teacher   22

   Studying with a Teacher vs.
      Using Method Books   23

   Studying Multiple Styles   23

   Choosing a Guitar Program   24

Fingernails and Calluses   25

   Playing with Fingernails   25

   Fingernail First Aid   26

   Caring for Calluses   26

   Bass-String Squeaks   26

Practicing   28

   Structuring Practice Time   28

   Using a Metronome   28

   Warming Up for Performance   29

   Taking a Vacation from the Guitar   29

Repertoire and Interpretation   31

   Basic Repertoire   31

   Keeping Abreast of New Music   31

   New Music for Classical Audiences   31

   Embellishing Composed Music   33

   Ensemble Playing   33

   Using Altered Tunings   35

   Handling Rests in a Score   35

Refining Techniques   37

   Harmonics   37

   Free Strokes and Rest Strokes   38

   Tremolo Exercises   40

   Stopping Open Strings   40

   Cross-String Ornaments   41

   Percussive Techniques   45

Roadblocks   46

   Breathing   46

   Making Faces   47

   Reading High Notes on the Staff   47

   Hand Fatigue   48

   Rebuilding Hand Muscles after Injury   49

Where Mind Meets Music   50

   Memorizing Tips   50

   Relaxation and Visualization for Performing   51

   Tripping over Mistakes   53

Making a Career   54

Approaching Music Publishers   54

Finding a Niche in the Classical World   54

Notes on Concert Programming   57

Concerti for Guitar and Orchestra Performed by Sharon Isbin   68

Nylon-String Guitar Makers   70

Salons and Shops Specializing in Classical Guitars   75

Organizations   76

Classical Guitar Education Programs   77

Books   80

Periodicals   81

About the Author   82

Selected Recordings by Sharon Isbin   84

Foreword

When Sharon Isbin reaches for her guitar, closes her eyes, and begins to play, her music casts a spell. From the very first notes, her deep immersion in the music and her practiced and precise touch on the instrument allow her to cut right to the heart of the piece she's playing—and of the listeners themselves. In those moments, it doesn't matter who the composer is or what style or genre the piece is in; the communication is pure, visceral, and transporting.

In addition to hearing Isbin perform, I've had the good fortune to work closely with her in my role as editor of *Acoustic Guitar*. Her Master Class column, in which she answered readers' questions, appeared in our premier issue in the summer of 1990 and in every issue for the next four years. Although Isbin is a "classical" guitarist, it became clear right away that as a writer she cut through the categories of style and genre just as she does as a player. Many of the issues that she discussed are equally applicable to a steel-string strummer and to an aspiring classical player. The readers of *Acoustic Guitar* picked up on this quality in Isbin's work right away, and what ensued were four years of wide-ranging and thought-provoking exchanges that form the basis of this book.

Reading over the 50 collected questions and answers in the *Classical Guitar Answer Book,* I'm struck by how much Isbin's commitment and caring shine through. There's a lot of inspiring advice to be found in these pages—as well as plenty of calls for hard work and dedication—that make me want to open my guitar case and get on with the quest of becoming a better musician. Onward and upward . . .

—Jeffrey Pepper Rodgers

Introduction

Doesn't *everyone* play the guitar? Whether it's folk, country, bluegrass, Latin, jazz, rock, or classical, it seems that just about everybody strums, picks, or plucks a little. There are more than 15 million guitar players in the United States alone. The guitar is the most commonly owned instrument in America; it adorns the richest and the poorest of households, standing as a proud symbol of culture that transcends all class boundaries.

Why is the guitar so popular? It is an ideal instrument of self-expression, and unlike most other instruments, it sounds complete without any accompaniment. Cradled in your lap, the guitar becomes an extension of your physical being and soul. Its gentle tone offers a soothing refuge from the cacophony of modern life, and you can take it anywhere. The guitar also brings people together. As a partner in chamber music, its harmonic, melodic, and rhythmic strengths provide a beautiful complement to voice and other instruments.

Whether you play guitar as a hobby or professionally, the more you know, the better you become, and the more joy music can bring to your life. Success requires not only a love of music, but dedication and discipline. Everyone has at least some degree of talent, and the keys to realizing that talent are knowledge and hard work. If you wish to achieve your full potential, you must learn as much as possible about technique, practice skills, interpretation, memorization, performance psychology, and music in general. As you develop your skills, you'll gain the confidence and ability to take on new challenges and reach higher goals.

Being a great player, however, is about much more than just technique. You also must have something special and compelling to say. Though artistic personality can't be taught, you can cultivate the qualities that allow it to flourish: curiosity, a sense of adventure, creativity, sensitivity, and integrity. A skillful and intelligent guiding hand is important early on, as is wisdom and care in advanced study. One must never stop being a student and must always remain open to learning from the infinite world of life's experiences.

In the pages that follow, I take great pleasure in sharing some of the knowledge, insight, and secrets I've uncovered in more than 30 years of performing and teaching. May this book open new doors of potential and understanding, and challenge and inspire you to seek ever higher levels of music making.

—Sharon Isbin

Equipment

What specific qualities do you look for when choosing a guitar?

The instrument I select must be able to respond to a wide variety of musical demands, from the contrapuntal complexities of a Bach fugue, to exotic tone contrasts in contemporary music, to the sensuality of Spanish music. When trying out a new guitar, test it in the following categories, first abstractly and then while playing different pieces:

Beauty of tone. Does the guitar speak with a voice that is yours? Can you create a melting, luscious sound? If not, this marriage won't last long. *Dynamic and timbral contrasts.* Can the sound whisper as well as wail? Is it sharp and metallic by the bridge, sweet and dolce near the top of the fretboard? *Clarity and speed of response.* Clarity is important because it is a component of projection and speed. Are notes well articulated and crystalline in fast passages, with a quick response, or is the effort dull-sounding and labored? *Sustain.* To achieve lyrical, legato playing, sustained vibration is the key. To test this, count how many seconds individual notes remain audible. From note to note (on a single string), the count should be fairly consistent and long enough to make slow melodic works truly connected and singing. *Balance.* Also necessary for lyrical playing, balance is the equality of sound from note to note and string to string. When playing notes in a chromatic sequence or in scales that change strings, the transitions should be smooth and seamless. Try playing various melodic works to see if the line is well shaped. In contrapuntal music, are the different voices clear? Chords, too, must sound well integrated. A good test is Fernando Sor's Study #9.

Resonance. I would describe resonance as the quality of richness and depth that makes one guitar sound three-dimensional, vibrant, and full-bodied, and another sound as flat as champagne tastes the morning after. *Intonation.* To check the intonation, first make sure the strings are even and of a high quality. Notes played at the 12th fret should be equal in pitch to those played as harmonics. Tune the guitar from string to string, then check using harmonics, skipping several strings. If the pitches are inconsistent, or the instrument plays in tune only in one key, put it back on the rack. *Projection.* This bane of most guitars is best tested in a concert hall; first play the instrument yourself and then hear others play it. If a hall audition is not possible, a large room will give you some idea of the instrument's carrying power, especially if you can compare it to other guitars. Don't worry about projection, however, if you never intend to play outside your own four walls. *Condition.* Avoid guitars with back-bowed or overly warped necks. You can spot these problems by peering down the edge of the neck with eyes level at the bridge. Also, nasty-looking cracks that have not been properly sealed spell trouble. Personally, I wouldn't touch a new guitar that has any cracks, and I certainly would not seek out an old guitar that has more than a couple of benign cracks. Steer clear of tops that are significantly caved-in near the bridge. Otherwise you might be awakened in the middle of the night by a major explosion.

Equipment

Comfort. Finally, the instrument should feel comfortable. Remember that some problems are correctable. An uncomfortably thick neck can be shaved by a luthier, and old, worn frets can be replaced. Distances between strings can sometimes be adjusted. If the action (distance from strings to neck) is too high, lower it at the bridge and/or nut to a point just before buzzing would occur and see if it is now easy to play. (A back-bowed neck will sabotage any respectable effort.) If you raise the action, be sure the bone has enough support and does not tilt to any major degree. Don't count on changing the neck length, however. Longer neck lengths, such as in Ramírez guitars, may be fine for some people, but torture for others. Young children or adults with unusually small hands will need guitars built on a smaller scale than the norm. But don't wait too long to figure out that the instrument was really built for a Goliath—by then you may already have fallen in love with it!

Why are classical guitars offered in various scale lengths? I have seen them as low as 630 millimeters and as high as 665. What is the standard length, and how do I determine what length is right for me?

Scale lengths vary to accommodate both builder and player preferences, as well as the different sizes of players' hands. The definition of "standard" has changed considerably in the last few years. In the 1960s and '70s, 664 mm was a common string length, largely due to the influence of the Ramírez factory in Spain. Now even the Ramírez company is making shorter-scale guitars. When I got my 1988 Thomas Humphrey Millennium model, Humphrey was building most of his instruments at 660 mm, including the one I play. In 1993 he began building most of his instruments at 650, because many guitarists find the shorter length more comfortable for the left hand. The traditional belief is that only guitars with long string lengths can be loud and powerful. Humphrey and other makers disagree, and they are building shorter scales, which they claim do not sacrifice volume or timbre.

If a child is going to study classical guitar, it is important that the width, body size, and string length be comfortable. Stretches should not strain the left-hand wrist or fingers. A child must also be able to hold the instrument securely, with adequate right-hand mobility. Some years ago, Japanese luthiers created a wide range of guitar scales to accommodate children as young as three or four. This was no doubt inspired by the success of the Suzuki method for violin and cello. (My sister, in fact, was one of the early U.S. Suzuki "pioneers" and started violin at age three and a half on what was called a "one-eighth size.") When I was nine years old and about to begin guitar studies in Italy, my teacher sent me to Mario Pabé, a maker in a nearby farm village. He measured my hands and within a few weeks built me a smaller-bodied guitar with a string length of 655 mm. I used it for a couple of years before graduating to a larger instrument.

Since I have long fingers, my choice of string length as an adult is strictly a matter of preference. A guitar with a 664 mm scale length doesn't give me the flexibility of a 660

Equipment

mm, so I avoid the former. Some adults have unusually small hands and would be better off with scales below 660 mm. Others have especially thick fingers and need more space between strings than many smaller-scale models provide. Neck thickness (which can be reduced) and width, as well as body length and width, vary from model to model and also influence how comfortable the instrument feels. An excessively high action will make playing any guitar difficult, so first see that your instrument is properly set up.

If you are choosing an instrument, try out your most difficult pieces, including those with challenging stretches, on guitars with different scale lengths. Give yourself enough time on each to determine compatibility. If you are a beginner, ask your teacher for advice. And use common sense: if you have unusually small hands, don't seek out a 664 mm behemoth!

Do you prefer a guitar with a cedar or a spruce top?

I sometimes find that spruce tops are more versatile than cedar tops in their ability to perform well for all types of repertoire. The clarity and evenness they offer, for example, is essential when playing Baroque music and is often hard to come by with cedar. Cedar, on the other hand, can sometimes have an edge over spruce when it comes to a melting depth and warmth of tone for Spanish music. The ideal is to find an instrument with both of these qualities *and* a strong projection.

What do you think a performing guitarist should know about instrument care and repair?

A guitarist should know how to prevent damage from exposure to the elements and from impact and should have rudimentary skills in cleaning, repairing faulty machine heads, solving action problems at the nut and bridge, and fixing minor electronic glitches if using a built-in pickup.

Prevention is always the best medicine. In very cold or hot weather, keep the guitar in a climate-controlled area. A common mistake is to place it in the trunk of a car, which can be devastating when it means exposure to temperature extremes. When the instrument is outdoors, avoid direct contact with sunlight. You can't exactly slather it with PABA SPF 25, so rather than risk cracking (hot mountain sun can cause cracks within minutes!), stay in the shade.

When traveling in dry climates, clip one or two cello Damp-Its in the soundhole (when the guitar is in its case, you should lodge them between the first two treble strings for a sturdier hold). Squeeze and wipe the Damp-It thoroughly to ensure that it won't drip inside the guitar. Avoid moistening the area by the Damp-It's clip so as not to expose the wood to direct contact with water. Be sure to remove the Damp-It(s) while performing, because they muffle the sound and often produce buzzes.

Equipment

Basic maintenance also includes cleaning the body, neck, and fingerboard. Grime buildup on the fingerboard, for example, can slow down your left-hand shifting. Consult a guitar maker to determine the best cleaning polish to use on your guitar's finish. If playing flamenco or using a pick, protect the soundboard from dents by affixing a plastic pickguard. Since pickguards can alter the sound, I recommend cutting one or two to size and attaching them temporarily with four loops of removable tape.

Keep the guitar in a solid case, preferably one with a slightly arched top. Soft cases offer little protection from impact and place your instrument at risk. Even when you think it's safe turf at home, it's best to store the instrument in a closed case. Nocturnal wanderings, wind from open windows, and earthquakes can all wreak havoc. I once knew a performer who knocked over a vaporizer in the middle of the night. The next day while practicing, he felt water trickling down his thigh. He discovered to his horror that the vaporizer had emptied its water into the soundhole and the water had saturated the wood, loosening all the seams. The guitar was ruined.

Even if you have a good case, be on guard for faulty handles or straps. Few cases would allow your instrument to survive unscathed if they suddenly lurched from your hand or shoulder onto hard pavement. Finally, don't check your guitar in airline baggage unless you have a heavy-duty travel case and are assured it will be handled gently. If you do check it, loosen the strings to avoid strain from unpressurized cabins.

In the event of an emergency, a few repairs are feasible to do on your own. If the action has changed and is creating buzzes or uncomfortable tension, make appropriate adjustments at the bridge and/or nut. Carry extra bridges and nuts along that are slightly higher and lower than what you're using. That way, if the neck's bow changes, you can make a replacement. You can also sand down a high bridge or nut on the bottom side. Low bridges and nuts can be raised with a wood shaving (in the event that you don't have a thin sheet of wood handy, you can slice a shaving off a long wooden matchstick), provided the slot in which it fits is deep enough to hold it stable. If a single groove has worn too deeply in the nut, you can repair it temporarily by layering on Krazy Glue until the groove depth matches that of the others.

If your machine heads break, replace them by removing the strings and unscrewing the old heads. If the problem is a squeaky or stiff gear, a little oil may solve the problem. If a gear is stiff because a screw is pulling away from the neck and causing misalignment, try replacing the screw. If you still can't get traction, wedge tiny wood shavings into the hole until the screw will stay firm. This is a temporary measure until your guitar can be fixed professionally. If you use a built-in pickup, carry along extra batteries and a miniature screwdriver. It would also be wise to carry an extra pickup in case your built-in pickup stops working. Finally, I wouldn't attempt to repair cracks. That kind of work is best left to a professional.

Equipment

What can cause a rattle in a guitar?

Strings, loose joints and bracings, loose frets, dried glue, cracks, and foreign objects are some of the major potential culprits in the case of a mysterious rattle. But before pulling out mirrors and flashlights to investigate the interior of your guitar, check for more obvious problems.

First, shake the guitar vigorously. Is there a rattle inside the soundbox? Turn the guitar upside down so that the soundhole faces the floor and shake again, tipping slightly from side to side. If there is a loose object, it should eventually tumble out. When this happened to me a few years ago, I was horrified to witness the hardened corpse of a roach fly out and land on the floor. Ensnared by Vivaldi and Rodrigo, it hadn't had a meal in days and had been transformed into a pathetic percussive accoutrement.

Check the bridge area to see if any of your strings is resting on the soundboard. On a classical guitar, long string-ends left to rest on the wood will surely rattle away like a snare drum. In order to keep the ends short yet secure, you should thread the string once or twice through its loop before putting it out through the bridge hole. In the case of treble strings, tie small knots at the very ends to assure that they can never snap through the holes. (This isn't necessary with carefully affixed bass strings because their metal windings inhibit slippage.)

Check the tuning peg area to see if any string ends are rattling, either against the wood or against other strings. Play open strings with your right hand while damping suspicious targets with your left. If the rattle stops at any point, you've probably found the source. Similarly, check for loose pegs and machine heads by applying pressure to each as you play.

Check carefully for cracks throughout the instrument. If you find one, press it while playing open strings. If the rattle stops, the crack should be glued by a professional repairperson.

Play open strings and move your left hand around the soundboard, including all edges, applying pressure inch by inch. If you don't get any results, apply pressure to the area of the neck that covers the soundboard and the bridge. If that doesn't work either, try the back and sides. Then try pressing each fret. If at any point the rattle stops, the pressure point indicates the probable area of trouble—most likely a loose joint, loose glue, or an interior crack. Once you've identified the area, you can investigate further with a mirror and a flashlight, but the problem will still require professional repair.

If the rattle occurs only on specific pitches that are not open strings, you'll need an extra arm to help. Strike the afflicted pitch while someone else moves his or her hands over the soundboard, back, sides, etc.

If after all this you still haven't solved the puzzle, you might consider having your ears checked!

Equipment

Do you recommend regular-tension or high-tension nylon strings?

String tension is a matter of personal taste and suitability for each instrument. I prefer high-tension bass strings because they project well and are less likely to buzz. With treble strings, the issue is more complex because there are many varieties of thickness, density, rigidity, and tension currently available. (Some of the popular brands are Augustine Regal and Imperial, and Savarez Red and Blue Alliance.) These factors influence projection, clarity, speed, timbre, sustain, vibrato, and comfort.

To decide which treble strings work best on your instrument, I recommend testing three different brands of the same string simultaneously. With three E's as the first three strings, for example, you can readily compare all of the characteristics I mentioned above. I have found it helpful and fun to share the task with a jury of blindfolded friends. After three hours of hearing only E strings, however, I must admit I thought I was losing my mind. And anyone who might have walked in on the scene would have been certain of it. But the experiment did answer some important questions.

How often do you change strings?

I change bass strings just before they start to buzz, unravel, or turn dull, and I change treble strings when they're about to become scratchy, muted, or out of tune from stretching or fret indentations. How often does that happen? It depends upon what and how much I'm practicing and upon the demands of my performance and recording schedules.

Many factors affect string wear and tear, and for bass strings that includes altered tunings, chemistry, and climate. For example, lowered bass tunings (such as the sixth string at D or C, or the fifth string at G) tend to sound dull sooner than the standard tuning (sixth at E, fifth at A). A lot of switching back and forth between tunings helps to wear out the strings as well.

And don't underestimate chemistry in the assault against bass strings. Luckily, my hands rarely sweat, and if they do, there doesn't seem to be any of the destructive component that plagues some players. In a normal routine of three to four hours a day of practice, I can often use unpolished bass strings for two weeks at a time (polished basses for recording last about a day, however). Players whose hands sweat a lot can go through a new set of bass strings every day or two. (Knowing that may make you think twice about letting anyone try your guitar!) Humid climates also increase the sweat factor. In any case, frequent hand washing temporarily rids fingers of oil and dirt and will extend the life of bass strings.

In long-term use of bass strings, you may also need to guard against unraveling, which leads to breakage. Check the bridge area when you first install the string. If there is a space between the coils at the bone or at the juncture with the curved portion of the

Equipment

string, gently press and move the coils to redistribute them so there are no visible spaces. Do the same at the frets if coils begin to separate with use.

The biggest enemies of treble strings are right-hand fingernails, picks, fret pressure, and loss of pliancy. Normal nail use will create small scratches on nylon strings, and the problem is exacerbated by *rasgueado* striking techniques and picks. As the scratches increase, treble strings begin to sound raspy rather than smooth. This becomes particularly problematic in recordings. A good test of your scratch factor is first to smooth out your nail with fine-grade sandpaper, and then glide it lengthwise along the string. Compare the sound above the uppermost frets (in a smoothly finished string) with the sound over the soundhole area where you normally strike. If the string sounds unacceptably raspy, but is otherwise still in tune, resilient, full, and loud, you can continue to use it by unwinding it three inches or so and refastening and shortening it at the bridge. The scratchy patch will now be out of reach. Since tuning readjustment will be less of a problem than with a new string, this "recycling technique" is useful when there is little time between performances.

Normally, I can use treble strings for three months at a time. With such long-term use, however, I routinely check for any indications of unevenness in the strings' girth. Compare the 12th-fret pitch with its 12th-fret harmonic. If the pitches match, the string is still even (presuming, of course, that your guitar is properly fretted!). If not, change the string.

My performance schedule also influences when I change strings. Since strings require enough time to adjust so that they won't go out of tune in performances or during recordings, I pace myself accordingly. Whenever possible, I allow ten days for new treble strings to settle in before a performance, and three days or so for bass strings. If I am recording with unpolished bass strings, I allow a week for them to stretch out and become less squeaky. If recording with polished basses (such as La Bella 413P Studio Strings, which don't squeak and require hardly any adjustment time for tuning), I change them the night before each session.

Why do classical guitarists use footrests? Can I play in a classical style without using one?

Using a footrest under the left foot allows the guitar to rest securely on both legs. The weight of the right arm provides a counterbalance so that no effort is required to keep the instrument motionless while playing. In this position, one can make fast left-hand leaps with precision and maintain right-hand accuracy and dexterity because the guitar remains still. The angle of the fingerboard creates optimal conditions for keeping your back straight and for finding a comfortable left-hand position (a horizontal neck would strain the wrist and limit mobility). Playing with one foot flat on the floor and your legs crossed is not as secure and will also make fingering in higher positions more difficult. It might also encourage circulation problems, such as varicose veins.

Equipment

For those players who must keep both feet flat on the floor because of back problems, devices such as cushions and suction cups have been developed to elevate the guitar. The only problem with these is that the guitar tends to wobble during position shifts. When this happens, both right- and left-hand fingering become more treacherous. The right arm may also have a tendency to tense up in an effort to apply more weight to stop the motion. An alternative that can improve stability somewhat is to use a very low footstool in conjunction with one of these elevating devices. One can certainly play in a classical style without a footstool or device that raises the guitar if the pieces don't have rapid or demanding shifts. Anything complex, however, will be problematic when you're hunched over or teetering.

Do you use amplification in performance?

I usually use sound enhancement when playing solo or chamber music in halls that seat more than 700, and I always use it when performing with an orchestra. I use the minimum amount of volume necessary so as to maintain the intimacy and beauty of the instrument. Though it is certainly possible to project forcefully without amplification in large halls, I prefer instead to retain a large dynamic range, a diverse palette of timbral colors, and all the subtle nuances, such as sensuous portamentos (sliding wisps of sound between notes)—much of which is lost when projection becomes the primary concern.

The system I now use was designed for me by two engineer/musicians, Elias Guzman and Bruce Hildesheim. The extraordinary thing about their invention is that no one in the audience is aware that the guitar is amplified. There is nothing to see, because the tiny wireless microphone and battery hook under the soundhole, and the bookshelf-sized wooden box containing two Celestion speakers, a Rane 15-band graphic equalizer, and a Shure wireless receiver and amp is hidden (either behind a curtain, behind the shell, camouflaged against a wall, or within the orchestra). The speaker is also powered by a small battery pack, so no wires or plugs are necessary. The mic fits onto any acoustic guitar and takes about 15 seconds to place. Volume adjustments are made with a small digital remote control that can be operated at the performer's chair. The box should always be placed at least six feet (and up to 15 feet) behind the performer.

The resulting sound is truly amazing. Thanks to a unique omnidirectional design, no matter where I am on stage, it always appears as if the sound is coming directly from the guitar. It is so completely natural, balanced, and absent of fingernail and string noises that everyone in the audience is fooled. When I first used the system in October 1993 playing John Corigliano's concerto with the St. Paul Chamber Orchestra in the Ordway Music Theater (1,800 seats), not even the critics knew. In recital, the benefits are equally inspiring. The system enhances the sound of a dry hall to make the listening experience much more rewarding for the audience. The orchestra managers and concert presenters who have heard it are astonished that the guitar can sound so clear and natural, and they claim that this is the first time they've heard it so in their many frustrating years of hearing traditionally miked guitars.

If you don't own this system and must rely on the hall to provide sound reinforcement, there are other alternatives. When playing solo, an excellent house system with a high-quality microphone (such as an AKG or a Sennheiser) can provide satisfactory sound enhancement. In situations where the amplification isn't audible on stage, you may wish to request a monitor. If there is no house system, two high-quality speakers can be placed against the side walls, about halfway back from the front of the stage, facing each other (not the audience). Work with the engineer before the performance to make the sound as natural as possible. This involves careful attention to the balance of the bass, treble, and midrange, and avoiding a boomy bass or a tinny treble.

When performing concertos with an orchestra, I used to request a very specific setup. It consists of a directional microphone (rather than an omni to avoid any bleeding from the orchestra) placed on a boom stand near the bridge. Two small speakers (such as Bose 802s or 803s, Meyers, or Apogees) are mounted on two eight-and-a-half-foot adjustable poles and placed next to each other in the center of the *back* of the stage, behind the orchestra. The engineer should be prepared to mix this sound, if necessary, with a slight amount of the house speakers, with the percentage of house usage not to exceed ten to 20 percent of the total.

Before the rehearsal starts, work with the engineer to establish basic levels of equalization and volume. The engineer should make further adjustments during the rehearsal. Be sure the board is set up within the hall or in a booth with an open window so the engineer hears what the audience will hear and can make final adjustments during the performance. I find it helpful to hear another guitarist play for a few moments on stage so I can listen from the hall.

This format has a few of the benefits of the system designed by Guzman and Hildesheim. With the speakers placed behind the orchestra, the conductor, the players, and soloist all hear the solo part clearly and can interact accordingly. Because the speakers are mounted on poles several feet high, the volume on stage is never excessive. When the sound reaches the audience, it has been acoustically enhanced by the stage, just as the sound of the orchestra has been enriched before it reaches the audience. Best of all, what the audience hears appears to come more from the guitar than it would if using a ceiling or wall unit.

In this day and age of high-quality equipment, there is no excuse for bad amplification. Unfortunately, most guitarists do not know what to request, and as a result many conductors and orchestra managers have become soured on the idea of using guitars. The mistake most engineers and guitarists make is either to project exclusively through the

Equipment

ceiling cluster, turning the sound into a circus of artificiality, or to rely on upstage side speakers, which split the sound in two and blast the first few rows of listeners. Either way, the sound is schizophrenically detached from the soloist. And often the orchestra can't hear a note the guitarist is playing.

What precautions should I take to protect my guitar when I travel?

Carry your guitar in a strong, sturdy case. It should have a slight arch above the bridge area to allow a margin of safety should sudden pressure ever be applied to the top of the case. If you travel by air and check the guitar, use a large, extra-durable case, such as the fiberglass-reinforced model made by Mark Leaf (322 N. Ash, McPherson, KS 67460). Since baggage compartments are not always pressurized, loosen the strings before flying. Lock the case, affix plenty of "Fragile" stickers, and try to arrange for special handling pickup and delivery at the gate (a growing improbability with increased airport security regulations). Since luggage is frequently lost or damaged, I would recommend that you insure your guitar for its full value.

Another option when traveling by air is to use a regular-sized case and buy an extra seat. Since airlines have various restrictions about where instruments can sit, it is best to make these arrangements adequately in advance.

The third alternative is to try to store your guitar on board. If you plan to do this, be sure that the overhead bins are large enough to accommodate a normal-sized case or that there is unmotorized closet space ("motorized" closets are made for lightweight garment bags, not for guitars).

When traveling to dry climates, always take along a couple of Damp-Its (sponges enclosed in rubber tubes). After wetting the Damp-It, squeeze it out and dry the outside of the tube thoroughly. Anchor it between two treble strings at the soundhole. Clipping it on the wood can damage the finish, and it is likely to fall off and bounce around inside the guitar.

Since carrying the case with a shoulder strap is convenient, some cases have metal loops at each end where the strap can be attached. If you use this system, be sure that the strap is securely fastened before you throw it over your shoulder. I'll never forget the time I got out of a car, lifted the case, placed the strap on my shoulder, and watched in horror as the case smashed onto the sidewalk. A 16-inch crack in the guitar was my reward for being careless.

I can't seem to get my guitar to sound in tune. I realize that tempered tuning is a compromise for all keys and that a guitar can't be truly "in tune" everywhere on the neck, but is there a tuning method that gives the best compromise?

Presuming that the frets on your guitar are properly spaced, the first thing to check is the condition of each string. Play a harmonic on the 12th fret and then finger the same fret. (Never use vibrato when tuning.) If the pitches are identical, the string is probably even in thickness and consistent in pitch. If the pitches differ, the string could be the culprit, or your guitar's intonation might need adjustment.

Next, tune the high E string to a tuning fork. (I use either A or E above the staff.) To keep the string from slipping, always tune up from a lower pitch to the desired pitch when making the final adjustment. Play a fifth-fret harmonic on the B string and tune it to the seventh-fret harmonic of the E string. Or finger the fifth fret on the B string and match it with the open E. A third check is to play the 12th-fret harmonic on the second string and match it with the seventh position on the first string.

Once the first two strings are in tune, finger the fourth fret of the G string and tune it to the open B. Then play a 12th-fret harmonic on the third string to be sure it is in tune with the third fret on the first string.

Tune the A string next by playing a harmonic on the seventh fret and matching it with the open E. Check the A string by comparing a harmonic on the 12th fret with the second fret of the G string.

Adjust the D string until its seventh-fret harmonic is identical to the fifth-fret harmonic of the A string. Check that the fifth-fret harmonic on D is in tune with the seventh-fret harmonic on G. Check again by playing a seventh-fret harmonic on D while fingering the fifth fret of the first string. Finally, check the harmonic on the 12th fret of D against the third fret of the B string.

Tune the low E by matching its fifth-fret harmonic with the open first string. Check that the open B is still in tune by comparing it to the seventh-fret harmonic on the low E string. Also compare the fifth-fret harmonic on the low E string to the seventh-fret harmonic on the A string, and the 12th-fret harmonic on the low E string to the second fret of the fourth string.

The last step is to check tuning as it relates to the piece you are about to play. If the piece is tonal, strum the tonic chord. Make any final adjustments necessary to be sure the chord is in tune. In pieces that link unison pitches on different strings, check the tuning of each unison. For example, make sure that all the E's match in the opening of Bruce MacCombie's *Nightshade Rounds,* or that the three E's in the arpeggio section of Etude #11 by Villa-Lobos are in tune. Conspicuous octaves should also be in tune, such as the octave E's that precede that arpeggio section.

If you are tuning on stage, speed and subtlety are essential. Tune as quickly and quietly as possible so the audience doesn't have to suffer through it. For minor adjustments, you can streamline the above to just the 12th-fret harmonic/adjacent string checks, followed by the piece excerpt. The speediest way to change a tuning is first to memorize the appropriate number of turns each peg requires in order to land at the new pitch. If you are changing to a lower pitch, tune down at least a half step lower than necessary, then tune up to the pitch you want. If you are going to a higher pitch, tune to the pitch, pull on the string firmly with your right hand to stretch it, and tune up once again. If you are using only a capo to change pitches, be sure to check the tuning of each string once the capo is in place since it often slightly alters the interval relationship between strings. If a string is only slightly sharp or flat, you can often save time by not using the machine head: pull gently to loosen a string, or press behind the nut to tighten it.

How should I hold the guitar so that I feel comfortable playing all the way up the neck?

In the basic playing position (which shouldn't change except when you encounter large left-hand stretches or special effects in the right hand), the guitar is supported without any muscular tension. The left foot lies flat on a footstool, and the curve of the guitar rests on the left thigh (or on a cushion or frame if you use one instead of a stool). Your right arm provides the counterweight.

To find its ideal position, allow your right arm to hang freely at your side. Raise it slowly and rest your forearm, just before the elbow, on the edge of the guitar's upper curve. Let your hand fall naturally above the strings, keeping the wrist slightly arched. To find your ideal left-arm position, drop your arm and let it dangle freely. Then move the forearm upward and grasp the neck. Your elbow should hang downward, guided only by the force of gravity. Except when fingering awkward stretches, maintain this natural position of the elbow.

When playing below the 11th fret, it is generally best to keep your back straight while leaning forward slightly. Your shoulders should also be straight, forming a line both perpendicular to the spine and parallel to the hips. Keep your shoulders relaxed and resting in the natural position created by gravity. Though rhythmic shoulder movements are occasionally appropriate—such as while playing syncopated Latin American music—do not otherwise raise your shoulders, and never in gestures that would produce tension. Keep your neck relaxed and in alignment with your spine. Though it is fine to move your neck horizontally (left and right), avoid bending it downward.

When playing above the tenth fret, it won't work to keep your back and shoulders straight. If you reach that high on the neck, your forearm tugs at your wrist, and finger motion is restricted. Your hand feels terrible. When you move from approximately the 11th fret on to higher positions, the solution is to lower your left shoulder gradually while increasing the forward lean. Your hand should now feel relaxed and compliant. When returning from a higher position back to the 11th fret, gradually straighten your back until your body is in alignment once again.

Starters

Should a left-handed person play guitar left-handed?

I don't believe there is only one correct way to play if you are left-handed. I have seen some left-handed people play right-handed with no trouble, and some who had played right-handed for an extended time switch to left-handed because they found it easier. Before ordering a specially built guitar in which the inside bracing is altered to accommodate the reversed string order, experiment with playing right-handed.

To speed up this decision-making process, you could practice for an equal amount of time each day the same exercises and pieces right-handed on your regular guitar, and then left-handed on a second guitar whose strings have been reversed. Within a relatively short period of time, it should become clear which position is more comfortable for you.

At what age do you think a child can start learning —and enjoying—the guitar, and what should I look for in an instrument for a child?

Proponents of the Suzuki method will say that a child can begin to learn the piano or a stringed instrument as early as age three or four. Because Suzuki methods have now been developed for the guitar, a kid *can* start studying soon after shedding diapers. Young children learn by rote for the first few years, and with constant parental supervision. Is this desirable? It depends on the personalities of the child and the parent involved. Though such close-knit interaction may work well in a country like Japan where the Suzuki method was first developed, it often presents problems and power struggles in our more independence-oriented culture.

If the parent doesn't want to get involved in practice sessions and lessons, then she or he should wait until the child is at least six or seven (I started at age nine). Whether using Suzuki materials or not, it helps to have an excellent recording the child can listen to of all the musical examples that she or he encounters.

Whatever the parent and child decide, they should be sure to choose a good teacher. If a kid learns bad habits at a young age, it is very difficult and frustrating to unlearn those habits later on.

As for the instrument, a child under the age of 11 or 12 will require an undersized instrument. The teacher should advise the parent which of several ready-made sizes would be appropriate, based on the child's finger and arm length.

Do you think beginning guitarists should learn to sight-read single notes before learning any chords?

It depends upon your individual goals. If you want to study folk guitar, start by learning chords. If you want to concentrate on classical guitar, it is best to learn individual notes first for a variety of reasons. You will be able to read more quickly, and you will also have the opportunity to develop good right- and left-hand techniques more conscientiously. It is easier to concentrate on both a good left-hand position and a proper free and rest stroke form in the right hand when you are learning only one note at a time, rather than a cluster of notes.

Concentrating on single notes also allows you to practice the alternation of right-hand fingers, a technique essential for developing finger independence. This sort of practice is conducive to learning rhythmic notations as well.

What qualities should I look for in a guitar teacher, and how should I go about finding one?

Since there are so many styles of guitar playing, it is important to find a teacher whose expertise reflects the style you wish to study (classical, jazz, folk, bluegrass, flamenco, etc.). If you are seeking classical or jazz instruction, phone the music department of your local university or conservatory to see if there is a guitar department. Speak to the department head and inquire about private lessons. The instructor should be able to evaluate your needs and make other recommendations, if necessary. If there is a local guitar society, the president and board members would also be good sources of information about local instructors.

There are various ways to evaluate the musical and technical potential of a teacher:

Inquire about the instructor's background. What degrees did she or he receive and with whom? Past instructors are potential indicators about a teacher's outlook and approach.

Listen to recordings or attend a performance. Do you relate to the style of playing? Does the playing reflect a thorough and disciplined knowledge of technique and musical styles?

Attend a master class. Talk to students to get an idea of their experiences with the instructor. This is important because not all fine performers are good teachers.

Once you have a candidate, arrange a lesson. Is the teacher attentive and interested, or bored and distracted? A teacher who is enthusiastic about music and problem solving will inspire and encourage you in your quest to grow. Seek out a teacher who is patient, articulate, communicative, and creative. If you ask questions, the answers should be thoughtful and illuminating, rather than dogmatic or superficial. A teacher should be willing to explain in depth the mechanics of a musical or technical challenge, the "whys" and "hows" of problem solving. After all, only through genuine understanding can you assimilate and apply new ideas and knowledge.

Discuss your goals and aspirations. Are you both in agreement about expectations and workload, frequency of lessons, cost, etc.? If you wish to focus on specific repertoire (such as contemporary, Baroque, or chamber music), is the instructor supportive, and does she or he have the necessary background? In the end, you must have confidence in the teacher's knowledge, integrity, ability to communicate, genuine desire to help you grow, and respect for your individuality.

What do you think is the proper balance between learning from a teacher and learning from books and methods?

Because hand position and tone production are so important and challenging when first learning classical guitar, one must start with a good teacher, no matter how explicit books and methods may be. If you intend to pursue guitar as a hobby, a few months of weekly lessons may suffice to set you off on the right track, with occasional checks thereafter as needed. Since it is easy for bad habits to appear unwittingly, it would be best to consult a teacher monthly or bimonthly and whenever addressing new techniques. A teacher can also provide motivation, encouragement, and discipline, making learning not only faster but more enjoyable.

If your goals are professional or you are striving for a genuinely high level of musical and technical sophistication, weekly lessons for many years are the norm.

At present I'm working from four guitar method books that cover different styles: classical, bluegrass, fingerstyle, and standard flatpicking. Do you think it's wise to take this broad approach, or would I be better off narrowing my focus and concentrating on one style?

If you have the interest, time, dedication, and energy to devote yourself to more than one style, I see no reason to limit your approach. It will also give you the opportunity to explore a variety of styles to see if one or two eventually inspire you more than others. You can always choose to narrow your focus later.

Instead of shuttling about between four teachers, however, try to find one very versatile instructor, or perhaps one for classical and one for the other styles. You'll need to make sure that learning one style doesn't cause you to distort hand position in another. For example, if you use your left-hand thumb to finger notes in bluegrass, you'll need to be extra conscientious when playing classical not to let your thumb bend inward or extend beyond the neck. Maintain rounded left-hand fingers when playing classical, even if other styles call for more extension. If you practice with a pick, you'll have to guard against a sloping right hand when playing classical, or against the tendency for the right-hand thumb to lodge itself behind the index finger instead of being extended off to the left.

Many of the jazz, bluegrass, fingerstyle, and even rock professionals I've met studied classical guitar at one time in order to improve their technique. And classical players who know how to improvise can use that skill to advantage in their approaches to programming and composition.

Starters

I am seeking a school, college, or university that has a musical program geared specifically toward the guitar, rather than the keyboard. Any suggestions?

When choosing a school, your top criterion should be the quality of the guitar instructor. Researching this can take you far and wide, since the College Board Music Service currently lists more than 1,000 colleges and conservatories in North America that offer programs in classical guitar (also see the list on page 77). Other than the Berklee school for jazz studies in Boston, I am not familiar with any major music programs whose specific focus is the guitar. That is actually fortunate, because one of the biggest problems of classical guitar study is that it is often insular, separated from the larger world of music. Such ghettoized programs breed players with little experience in chamber music and sparse knowledge of symphonic, vocal, and general instrumental repertoire. Familiarity with music of other instruments helps to inspire and inform a guitarist's playing.

It's also true, however, that the keyboard often plays too large and intrusive a role in guitar programs. For instance, many programs require that all music majors, including guitarists, achieve a minimum proficiency on the keyboard in order to graduate. This requirement makes sense for theory, composition, and conducting students, and for musicians whose instruments are not harmonically self-sufficient (voice, strings, winds, brass). But for guitarists, a keyboard requirement often means needless and dangerous torture. Long nails on the right hand force a guitarist to compromise hand position at the piano. Playing a few chords and practicing simple ear-training exercises is not a problem, but gearing up to play fast scales and Bach inventions requires hours of practice. With a distorted hand position, all this work can lead to serious injury, such as tendinitis.

Because the guitar is a richly harmonic instrument, it makes more sense to skip the heavy-duty keyboard work and incorporate harmonic studies onto the fingerboard; that's the approach I took in designing the guitar program at Juilliard, which does not require any keyboard proficiency or study. Teachers should have the knowledge and ability to apply principles of theory and harmony to their teaching of guitar repertoire. Too often, theory remains an abstraction. When taught with understanding and insight in actual music, however, theory illuminates structure, fingering, and interpretation.

Fingernails and Calluses

Is it possible to play without using fingernails?

Classical guitarists can play without using nails, but they should be aware that in doing so they are sacrificing certain possibilities of tone color and projection—all of which affect interpretation and musical presentation. The nail, when used alone or with the flesh of the fingertip, adds clarity to articulation and aids in projection, from the softest to the loudest passages. For example, a pianissimo passage played only with the flesh will sound fuzzy and indistinct, yet the same dynamic shaped with the nail projects beautifully, even in a large hall.

The nail is also useful in achieving a variety of timbral colors. By varying the angle of the attack, the amount of flesh used with the nail, and the position of the attack relative to the bridge and fingerboard, for example, a player can achieve an enormous, even orchestral spectrum of sounds, from metallic to hauntingly sweet. Without nails, the range is far more limited.

Players who question using nails because theirs are hooked or brittle and breakable should first determine if their problem is correctable, either by nutritional changes or by applying a hardener to the upper third of the nail. Extra care to prevent nail damage might also solve the problem: Wear gloves while doing carpentry, washing dishes, lifting heavy items, gardening, painting, or using harsh solvents; open doors and dial the telephone with your left hand. And don't pick any fights! Shape nails with a good file and use a fine grade of sandpaper (preferably the silicone-coated variety) daily to keep edges smooth.

If none of the above works, another option is to wear false nails or carefully shaped Ping-Pong–ball cuttings affixed with Krazy Glue. I once had a student who even used his wife's toenails! Keep in mind when using Krazy Glue that the glue contains cyanoacrylate. Consult your doctor or a chemist to determine the toxicity potential of this chemical when it is repeatedly absorbed into the skin. A more immediate hazard, of course, is that skin bonding can occur. That means you should apply the glue carefully to avoid gluing your fingers and hands together, or having the table become part of your anatomy.

For players without professional aspirations, gluing on nails may not be worth the bother or the health risk that could result from regular use. In such cases, simply enjoy nailless playing without being concerned about the demands of concertizing. After all, many famous 19th-century players, performing on gut strings in small halls, used only flesh.

Fingernails and Calluses

I tore a nail on the day of a show. What could I have done to fix it well enough to at least get through the gig?

If the nail is torn but still attached, I highly recommend the new Savarez Nail Making and Repair Kit, which includes a special self-adhesive silk, resin, and applicators. Or you can affix a patch of China Silk (made by IBD, Inc., and sold in the nail-repair departments of drugstores) with Krazy Glue on the top side of the nail. In order to preserve a good tone, wait a few minutes for the glue to harden and then sand the edge with 500-grade (or finer) silicone-coated sandpaper until it is perfectly smooth.

If you lost the nail, the Savarez nail kit shows you how to build another. Or you can cut to shape a Player's Nail (made by Balcan Music and Accessories, 67-11 Yellowstone Blvd. #1C, Flushing, NY 11375)—or a Ping-Pong–ball substitute—and affix it with Krazy Glue to the underside of your nail. Again, smooth the edge with sandpaper.

Avoid soaking the mended nail in water for any significant length of time. If the nail does get wet, treat it with another dose of glue to ensure that it will remain intact during the gig.

Do you have any advice about caring for left-hand fingertip calluses? I build up pads that catch on strings, tear off, and leave tender, painful fingertips.

This is a common problem, especially in climates that are particularly cold or dry. You can usually keep the calluses smooth and "catch-proof," however, if you file them lightly with an emery board whenever they begin to show signs of peeling or flaking. (It's best to do this when the calluses are dry rather than waterlogged.) In cases where the air is so dry that deep cracks or fissures form in the callus, try bathing the tips in Vaseline (covering them with a glove or Band-Aids) whenever you're not playing or not embarrassed to be seen. Be sure to wash everything off thoroughly before playing, however, or your guitar will have a very slippery neck. If your calluses are prone to fissures, treat them regularly before the problem starts.

How do you avoid, or at least diminish, squeaks in the bass strings?

You can avoid left-hand squeaks by preventing your calluses from scraping against the coils. There are three basic ways to do this: lift the finger, slide on the flat part of the finger pad, or slide at an angle on either side of the fingertip.

Lifting is a viable option *only* if it does not disrupt the lyricism of a line, or if you don't wish to play a portamento (a connective wisp of sound between two notes). To lift without squeaking, raise the finger in a perpendicular line just high enough to clear the string, and then shift in an arclike motion to the next note. Any initial motion short of 90 degrees will brush against the coil and cause a squeak. If you shift one or more fingers on a treble string, slide on the string(s) in order to keep the hand anchored.

The flattened–finger-pad approach is ideal in situations where you want a portamento on one string but don't want the adjacent string to ring. When sliding, the finger can be either parallel to the frets, at an upward angle, or at a downward angle, depending

Fingernails and Calluses

upon what works best and is most comfortable for you in a specific situation. You can also slide on the pad of one finger and land on the tip of another, as in the opening of Prelude #1 by Heitor Villa-Lobos. Finally, if you choose to slide on the side of a fingertip, experiment with both sides to determine which is most comfortable.

The above techniques will be especially effective if you break in your bass strings for a day or two before a performance. Above all, listen for squeaks when you practice and get rid of them immediately. Many guitarists are so used to these extraneous sounds that they don't even hear them anymore, but nonguitarists are justifiably appalled by such creaking, grinding, and whistling.

Polished bass strings (such as La Bella 413P Studio Strings) work well for recordings but don't have the durability, clarity, and projection necessary for most concert performances. In certain performance circumstances, however, they may be adequate if projection is not an issue. Experiment with both polished and semipolished strings (such as those made by Savarez) to determine which sound best on your guitar. If you find a set that works, test its durability so you won't find yourself in the middle of a concert suddenly sounding dull and muffled, as if underwater.

If you decide to stay with normal bass strings, you can eliminate some of the squeakiness by lightly rubbing them with a high-grade sandpaper. Or dip your fingertips in talcum powder before playing pieces with squeaky passages. Powder will eventually dull the sound—just like dirt, oil, and grit do. But if you clean taut strings with a hot washcloth dampened only with water, you can extend their life for a few more days. It's best to clean them at full tension so as to reach all the spaces between the coils and ensure a stable tuning.

Finally, some players recommend soaking the last quarter inch of the fretting fingers in warm water for ten minutes and then drying them completely with a hair dryer (about 30 seconds) just before a performance. This technique could be particularly useful for people who are plagued with rock-hard calluses. If they become sticky after the treatment, try a little powder. If your fingertips become too soft, as after swimming, avoid playing for the next hour or two. When a callus becomes too weak and waterlogged, a pull-off slur can cause a blood vessel in your fingertip to burst. If this happens, it will leave you with a red, painful finger that could be useless for at least a week.

Practicing

When I practice, should I plan in advance exactly what exercises or pieces I will work on and how long I will spend on each?

It is always a good idea to plan a basic outline of each day's practice so that you use your time efficiently and accomplish what is necessary. This is especially important if you are preparing for a performance. Always allow at least 20 minutes (and up to an hour, if necessary) for initial warm-up exercises. This should include arpeggios, scales, and left-hand slurs. Allot sufficient time in each category to work up to your maximum tempo.

Then you should spend anywhere from ten to 30 minutes or more playing technically demanding studies and/or works in your repertoire, such as encore pieces, fast movements or variations from larger works, and pieces that are consistently fast and challenging to your stamina. This ensures a strong workout, even if you plan to spend the next few hours learning a slow saraband.

Estimate how many days, weeks, or months it will take you to prepare each piece, and pace yourself accordingly. You will need to establish daily goals as well as long-term goals. Since artistry and technical development are never totally predictable, however, be flexible. Being well organized makes the learning process even more enjoyable because you can focus thoroughly on each step, confident that it is part of an effective system that will fulfill your practice and performance needs.

Do you recommend practicing with a metronome? If so, how should I use one?

I definitely recommend using a metronome when practicing exercises that require speed development, such as scales, arpeggios, and slurs. Begin at a comfortable speed. Once you have mastered the exercise, increase the speed one notch at a time (or about two to four digits at a time, if you're using a numerical quartz meter). Advance to the next speed only when the previous one is perfect. Be sure that the notes are not only clear and accurate, but rhythmically even and synchronized precisely with the metronome beats.

This technique can also be extraordinarily useful when learning difficult scales or passages in compositions, or when learning entire pieces that are fast and rhythmically consistent. Villa-Lobos' Studies #1– 4, Barrios' Allegro from *La Catedral,* William Walton's fifth *Bagatelle,* Sagreras' *El Colibri,* and J.S. Bach's Allegro, BWV 998, are all excellent examples of complete works you can study with a metronome.

When practicing with a metronome, be careful not to become too rhythmically inflexible or mechanical. Always practice phrasing, breathing, dynamics, and articulation. Incorporate any ritards you have chosen by ignoring the metronome in those moments. Subdividing the metronome beats into smaller units permits such flexibility. When you have finished working on a piece, play it at least once without the metronome to rid your mind and fingers of any mechanical tendencies.

Practicing

When you're warming up before a concert, do you play the music that you're about to perform or do you play other music so that the program remains fresh?

That's an interesting question because there are so many different answers depending on the situation. If I'm playing solo music from memory, I prefer not to play any of it just before the concert. I warm up with scales and exercises and music that is not on the program.

If I'm playing a concerto and it's the first of several performances, I might choose to play through the piece again very softly an hour or so before the performance (playing softly, no matter what the repertoire, keeps the hands relaxed). If it's a world premiere, I'm even more likely to play through the piece an hour before the performance. When I premiered *Troubadours,* the beautiful concerto John Corigliano wrote for me and the St. Paul Chamber Orchestra, the ink was barely dry. I had memorized it in a short amount of time, and this approach helped to reinforce my focus and concentration.

I'd like to take more vacations without my guitar, but I'm torn between a desire for recreation and a fear of losing my chops. How long can one safely take off from playing without compromising ability?

You've spelled out a dilemma every musician faces: how to balance the discipline of playing an instrument with the desire to enjoy life away from your instrument too. It's pretty tough to backpack in the Rockies, cross-country ski in the Alps, or trek through exotic lands with a guitar slung over your shoulder. Does that mean a serious musician has to give up such pleasures? No, but one must choose time off wisely and be attentive to the ramifications.

I've found that when I don't play for a short period of time—up to three weeks—it takes an equal amount of time to regain what was lost. For example, if I don't touch the guitar for a week, I can expect to practice three or so hours a day for a week to regain my usual dexterity. To recover complete right-hand stamina may take even longer. I haven't taken longer than three weeks off, but if I did I assume it would take a proportionately longer time to get back up to speed, because the more time off, the more gradually one must return in order to avoid injury.

The telltale signs of deterioration are clear. Within a week, calluses diminish, stamina drops, and general muscle response becomes less controlled. To regain your skills as quickly as possible, practice scales, slurs, arpeggios, and technically demanding studies or short pieces. Don't pursue anything to the point of pain, however, because that will only provoke injury.

Another alternative is to set aside a little bit of time during your vacation to keep your chops up. An hour or even 45 minutes a day of vigorous scales, slurs, and arpeggios can significantly reduce the loss of technique. Since I love to take vacations that involve snorkeling, cross-country skiing, and trekking in remote wilderness areas, I've always dreamed of designing some type of practice fingerboard to accompany me.

Practicing

To my great delight, someone finally created a brilliant device for guitarists that is even better than the portable electronic keyboards that pianists use. It's called the SoloEtte Travel Guitar (available from Wright Guitar Technology, 3724 Gilham Dr., Eugene, OR 97408; phone/fax [541] 343-0872), and when disassembled for traveling, it's only 33 inches long and no wider than a guitar neck (see the "Travel Guitar" page on my Web site, www.sharonisbin.com). In less than a minute, you pop on three aluminum tubes designed to re-create the shape of an actual guitar. Your friends can't hear you practice, but you can by plugging earphones into a jack powered by a nine-volt battery. Since the nylon strings are tuned to pitch and the neck is identical to that of a real instrument, you can practice anything and experience the physical sensation of an actual guitar. A second model even plugs into an amplifier or sound system should you need to play a few gigs in between hikes. My first stop with the SoloEtte? I brought it to the Galápagos Islands and the Ecuadorian rain forest, and I am pleased to report that it worked wonderfully, surviving the rigors of dugout canoe travel, high humidity, and ravenous insects.

Repertoire and Interpretation

With regard to musical periods and composers, what should be in every guitarist's repertoire?

The Renaissance and classical periods are good starting points for beginners since it is easy to find relatively simple works in these eras. Examples of Renaissance composers are Milán, Narváez, Mudarra, Dowland, da Milano; a sampling of classical composers includes Sor, Giuliani, Carcassi, and Carulli. From there, one can branch out into other periods, such as the Baroque (Bach, Weiss, de Visée, Scarlatti), the 19th century (Tarrega, Paganini, Coste, Albéniz, Granados), the 20th century (Villa-Lobos, Barrios, Lauro, Llobet, Rodrigo, Turina, Torroba, Ponce, Tansman, Castelnuovo-Tedesco), and the contemporary (Brouwer, Henze, Britten, Dodgson, etc.).

Students should be exposed to a wide variety of styles and periods of history. If they later choose to specialize, they will at least have had a varied background on which to base such decisions.

How does one keep abreast of new music for guitar by contemporary composers?

For one of the most up-to-date catalogues of published guitar music, write to Guitar Solo, 514 Bryant St., San Francisco, CA 94107. You can also write to individual publishers and request their latest guitar catalogues. For a list of some of the many publishers who are active in contemporary guitar music, see page 54.

In addition, listen to (or at least read reviews about) concerts and recordings that include new music. There are two American publications that regularly review new guitar music: *Guitar Review* (40 West 25th St., 12th Floor, New York, NY 10010) and *Soundboard* (PO Box 1240, Claremont, CA 91711). The British monthly magazine *Classical Guitar* (Ashley Mark Publishing Co., 1 and 2 Vance Court, Trans Britannia Enterprise Park, Blaydon on Tyne, U.K. NE21 5NH; www.ashleymark.co.UK) is also a good source for new music reviews.

Music from contemporary composers has the reputation of being dissonant, "difficult," and unpopular with mainstream classical music audiences. In the guitar world, do you think audiences are resistant to new music, and if so, what can be done to improve this situation?

Just as not all Italian food is pasta, not all contemporary music is difficult and thorny. There are many different styles within the category of "contemporary," enough to offer a variety for all tastes. One can find everything from Afro-Cuban, Brazilian, jazz, bluegrass, Renaissance, and folk influences to more intellectual and "difficult" idioms. And within the realm of a particular category—such as atonal music—one can find a veritable panoply of approaches to lyricism, rhythm, texture, and color.

Harmonic delineations between tonal and atonal also vary considerably, not only between composers but within a composer's own body of work. Cuban composer Leo Brouwer, for example, has written in a variety of styles throughout his career. Compare his *La Espiral Eterna* (1971) to *El Decameron Negro* (1981). The harmonic, rhythmic, melodic, timbral, and structural language in these two works is strikingly different. And in concert, a distinguishing visual component is created by all the unusual performing techniques required in *La Espiral Eterna*. For example, there is a section that calls for the player to slither up and down the fingerboard and eventually sail past the frets toward the bridge. Visually and aurally, the effect is stunningly sensual. In another section, the performer taps in an improvised fashion with both hands on the fingerboard, creating the effect of a drummer in ecstasy.

Lack of familiarity with an individual work or compositional language may make it more difficult for some people to respond positively to a piece of music at first hearing. I remember hearing Benjamin Britten's *Nocturnal* for the first time some 30 years ago and thinking it was difficult music to enjoy. Now, however, having played it hundreds of times, I find it to be a beautifully moving and engaging work, written in a clear and accessible language.

I believe it is the performer's duty and responsibility to introduce audiences to outstanding 20th-century music. Unfortunately, not all performers have the background or sensibility to make sound judgments about quality and presentation. There have been many occasions when I have felt positively tortured by having to hear poorly written, uninspired, or defiantly antagonistic and abrasive music. But the wonderful works that do enter the literature are ample compensation.

Following the example of Julian Bream, who has been responsible for introducing many of the finest new guitar pieces (by such composers as Britten, Walton, Henze, Brouwer, Arnold, Berkeley, Takemitsu, and Tippett), I have also commissioned and premiered numerous solo and chamber works, including nine concertos with orchestra. These works include John Duarte's *Appalachian Dreams* (solo), Bruce MacCombie's *Nightshade Rounds* (solo, and version with string orchestra), Joan Tower's *Clocks* (solo) and *Snowdreams* (flute and guitar), Leo Brouwer's *El Decameron Negro* (solo), David Diamond's *Concert Piece* (guitar and string quartet), and with orchestra, Lukas Foss' *American Landscapes*, Joseph Schwantner's *From Afar*, Ivana Themmen's *Concerto for Guitar and Orchestra*, John Corigliano's *Troubadours*, Tan Dun's *Yi 2: Concerto for Guitar and Orchestra*, Aaron Kernis' *Double Concerto for Guitar and Violin*, Christopher Rouse's *Concert de Gaudi*, and Ami Maayani's *Concerto for Guitar and Orchestra*. (See Concerti for Guitar and Orchestra Performed by Sharon Isbin, page 68, and Selected Recordings by Sharon Isbin, page 84.)

Although I must confess that I've never been a fan of all-contemporary music concerts, the purpose they serve in giving new works the opportunity to be heard cannot be discounted. I prefer instead diversified programming, in which more familiar idioms offset the freshness and creativity of new works, and premieres aren't pitted against each other in a way that taxes both audience and critics.

Repertoire and Interpretation

How far do you think a performer can and should go in modifying or embellishing a piece of composed music?

A jazz, pop, or country musician is likely to answer that question differently from most classical players. Having heard exquisite jazz renderings of "composed" pieces from Bach to Ravel, I embrace the idea of truly improvised settings carried out with taste, skill, and creative artistry. It's when something is done halfway that expectations often become misleading and styles clash.

Some classical works actually require embellishment. For example, Bruce MacCombie's *Nightshade Rounds* and Leo Brouwer's *La Espiral Eterna* both require the performer to improvise certain passages. Cadenzas in solos, chamber works, and concertos have traditionally demanded input from the performer, especially in music written before the 20th century. Works by Haydn, Carulli, and Giuliani, to name a few, offer excellent opportunities for performers to write their own cadenzas.

Sometimes that practice extends to contemporary concertos as well. For example, in Joseph Schwantner's *From Afar* for guitar and orchestra, written for me and the St. Louis Symphony in 1988, the composer asked that I complete the second half of his cadenza (other soloists have the option of using my version or of creating their own); the same is true in Lukas Foss' concerto *American Landscapes*, written for me in 1989. In Baroque music, embellishment was expected. Modern players must apply principles of Baroque embellishment in order to avoid misrepresenting the composer's intentions. Failure to do so often leads to dull, inept performances.

Finally, when making transcriptions or arrangements within the classical music mode, modifications are usually necessary. The challenge, however, is to preserve the composer's original concept and intent while creating a setting that sounds completely idiomatic and natural on the guitar.

You've played with vocalists and a percussionist as well as with chamber groups and orchestras. Do you approach ensemble playing differently than you do solo playing?

Whereas solo playing gives total control to one player, ensemble playing demands an engaging interaction between musicians. A soloist is always in the forefront; an ensemble player must know when to lead, blend, or recede, according to the demands of the score. In an ideal ensemble, all performers listen to one another with a keen awareness, respond to each other's artistry, and breathe and move together in shared rhythms and phrases, mutual intensity, and beauty. It is a true union of soul and spirit, one whose physicality is unmatched by verbal forms of communication.

To achieve an expressive and dynamic unity, I seek musical partners who will relate to and complement my own artistic aesthetic. There must be honesty and open-mindedness in the process of working together, and a willingness and desire to explore new ideas and approaches. When rehearsing chamber music, all players should have the

Repertoire and Interpretation

ability to articulate thoughts and impressions with clarity and understanding. When there is disagreement, trust and respect will allow them to make intelligent choices and to support those decisions. And if a more convincing approach emerges later, performers should have the ability to recognize and embrace it.

Spontaneity is also a goal. One of the hallmarks of an exciting solo performance (where there are few limits), spontaneity is important in chamber and orchestral playing as well. Players must be ever sensitive to the moment and flexible enough to successfully create unplanned ideas or gestures. This is the magic that makes each performance alive and unique.

Since playing classical guitar means practicing and performing alone most of the time, it can be a joy to work with others, musically and socially. Some of the inspiring artists I've performed with include Nadja Salerno-Sonnenberg, Nigel Kennedy, Benita Valente, Carol Wincenc, the Emerson String Quartet, Carlos Barbosa-Lima, Larry Coryell, Laurindo Almeida, Michael Hedges, Herb Ellis, Stanley Jordan, Thiago de Mello, and, of course, many symphony orchestras and conductors. Ideas from colleagues rejuvenate and inspire, and often cross over to kindle new insight in solo repertoire as well. It is liberating to escape for a time from the confines of one's own thought process and be recharged with new artistic visions.

Because chamber and orchestral playing develops musical character in invaluable ways, it is an important part of my teaching at the Juilliard School. It introduces a new world of repertoire, most of which could never be played on solo guitar. When performing with others, one creates, in effect, a new instrument, one born of all the timbres and dynamics within the ensemble. These new colors and powerful dynamic levels expand the horizons of the guitarist to embrace everything from the human voice to an entire orchestra. This enlarged palette of color and lyricism has definitely enriched my playing, and it is a wonderful tool in teaching as well. Since chamber and orchestral music demand a rhythmic precision and awareness that is all too easy to ignore in solo playing, students learn rhythmic skills that can inform all their repertoire. My guitar students have the opportunity to perform an entire concert of chamber music every year in Alice Tully Hall at Lincoln Center. These ensembles have included guitar with voice, flute, oboe, percussion, piano, harp, mandolin, string quartet, and chamber orchestra.

Repertoire and Interpretation

In what situations do you change the tuning of your guitar for a composition—tuning the sixth string down to D, for example?

The most common tuning changes are: lowering the sixth string to D for works in D major or minor; changing the fifth string to G and the sixth to D for works in G major or minor; and changing the third string to F# for Renaissance lute works. I've also played with the sixth string tuned to C and with a capo on various frets (as on my *Love Songs and Lullabies* recording with soprano Benita Valente, baritone Thomas Allen, and percussionist Thiago de Mello, EMI/Virgin Classics 61480).

The most elaborate retuning I've come across requires that all strings be changed (C. Domeniconi's *Koyunbaba* is one example). In this case, you can either choose to wrestle with fate and watch your strings slip out of tune in this piece and/or in those that follow, or you can use two different guitars, each tuned accordingly hours ahead of time.

How do you handle rests in a guitar score?

A player should decide how to interpret a rest based on the musical and historical context of each situation. When playing transcriptions, for example, one must take into consideration the decay time of the different instruments. Because the guitar has a faster decay and a smaller sound than the piano or harpsichord, there are many times when it is desirable to allow a bass note on the guitar to ring through a rest. In the opening measures of J. S. Bach's "Prelude pour la Luth o Cembal" from the Prelude, Fugue, and Allegro (BWV 998), for instance, the keyboard notation indicates bass-note rests that do not sound convincing when played on the guitar.

Because the tonality remains constant throughout the measure, a guitarist can let the bass note decay naturally rather than stopping it abruptly on the third eighth note. This gracefully diminishing bass note reinforces the harmonic richness of both the instrument and the phrase. Without it, the upper voices float without a foundation. If one carries out this approach for the remainder of the piece, a sinuous beauty emerges that would be lacking if each rest were followed literally.

Repertoire and Interpretation

An example where it would be important, however, to stop the bass note on the rest is measure 54 from the Prelude of Bach's Suite BWV 996:

Since the new phrase begins on the second eighth note, it would only confuse the structure to allow the low G to continue ringing after the first beat.

Refining Techniques

How do you play harmonics?

When a note is written in the shape of a diamond or has a small *o* above it, it is meant to be played as a harmonic. There are two types of harmonics: natural and artificial. Natural harmonics are created by striking the string with the right hand while a left-hand finger presses lightly against the third, fourth, fifth, seventh, ninth, 12th, 16th, or 19th fret. The chart below shows what pitches you get from touching these frets on each of the six strings:

FIRST STRING

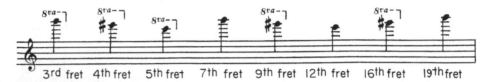

3rd fret   4th fret   5th fret   7th fret   9th fret   12th fret   16th fret   19th fret

SECOND STRING

fret: 3   4   5   7   9   12   16   19

THIRD STRING

fret: 3   4   5   7   9   12   16   19

FOURTH STRING

fret: 3   4   5   7   9   12   16   19

FIFTH STRING

fret: 3   4   5   7   9   12   16   19

SIXTH STRING

fret: 3   4   5   7   9   12   16   19

Refining Techniques

Clarity is important when playing harmonics. To be sure that your left-hand finger is pressing against the most resonant spot, move it slightly up and down from each fret while striking with the right hand. Carefully note the optimum location and try to hit it each time you play the harmonic. It will also help if your right hand strikes the string about midway between the edge of the soundhole and the bridge. You'll notice that the sound gets fuzzier and clunkier the further you venture toward the fretboard.

You can also create some of the pitches from the previous chart by playing above the 19th fret. Remove your left-hand finger from the string and touch the string lightly with the index finger of the right hand (over the soundhole and on toward the bridge) while striking the string with either your thumb or *a* finger (ring finger). Since there are no frets to guide you in this region, you have to estimate and experiment to find the sweet spot for your index finger to produce the harmonic.

You can create artificial harmonics by fingering the note an octave lower with the left hand (pressing against the fret as you would normally do when playing) and then touching the string lightly at its midpoint with the index finger of the right hand while striking with the thumb or *a* finger. You could create an F# harmonic on the first string, for example, by fingering the second fret with your left hand, touching at the 14th fret with your right-hand index finger, and striking that string. The *a* finger is generally easier to use than the thumb. But when playing bass strings, remember that the thumb is often more desirable because it won't scrape against the coils. Also, use a light touch with either technique to avoid excess nail noise.

How do you know when to play rest stroke instead of free stroke?

There are no set rules regarding rest and free stroke. In a rest stroke, the right-hand finger moves with a slight downward pressure onto the string it is striking and then continues in the direction of the string behind it. After "resting" momentarily on that string, the finger returns to its forward position for the next attack. Rest stroke with the thumb is similar, except that when it is combined with the return, the entire gesture creates a circular motion. Free stroke, however, is quite different. To avoid touching the adjacent string, one should move the finger upward at an angle toward the palm or wrist. If the finger moves upward in a vertical or perpendicular motion, the string will bounce vertically onto the frets and produce an ugly snapping sound.

If you were to ask ten professional guitarists to play the same piece of music, each would most likely use both strokes in totally different combinations. Also, an individual's interpretation often varies from one performance to the next. Each stroke produces a specific musical effect, and players not only differ in their musical goals but use their techniques in highly personal ways to achieve them. The issue is complicated further when you consider that there are also strokes in between free and rest, such as those

Refining Techniques

that lightly graze the adjacent string or that vary in their upward angle and distance from the string.

Projection, articulation, phrasing, rhythm, color, and musical character all influence one's choice of stroke technique. For example, since strong rest strokes are louder than strong free strokes, you might choose to use more of the former in situations where projection is important, such as when playing single lines and scale passages unamplified in large halls or with an orchestra.

While a series of loud, consecutive rest strokes can be very effective in passages requiring a percussive effect, in more melodic phrases it can sound crude and hammered, like a graceless dancer stomping about in hiking boots. For a truly legato and lyrical playing style, the overall majority of your strokes should be free stroke, with rest strokes used for textural variety, melodic and dynamic shaping, and rhythmic emphasis. When using both types of techniques (and their "in between" counterparts) within a phrase, the blend should be fluid, natural, and seamless. Do not use rest strokes when the adjacent strings must continue ringing, however.

To become technically adept at moving effortlessly from free to rest stroke (and vice versa), try the following exercise. When practicing it, keep your right hand still. Only your fingers should move. Use the chord progressions from Villa-Lobos' Etude #1.

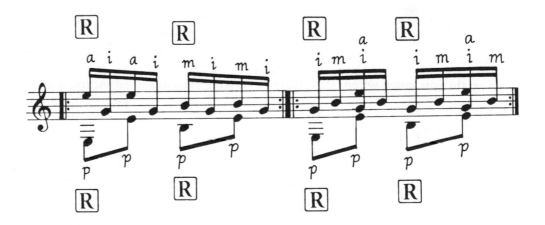

Keep your right hand relaxed. Play all notes with equal volume and good tone quality.

Though rest-stroke technique is generally associated with powerful projection, a very light, *piano* rest stroke can also create a beautiful effect. To hear this, place your hand over the soundhole and play four notes of a line softly, first free and then rest stroke. Also experiment with the amount of nail and flesh you use and the angle at which you approach the string. Since all of these factors influence your palette of colors, you should cultivate as fluent and versatile a right-hand technique as possible.

Refining Techniques

What exercises do you recommend for developing a strong tremolo?

Using the *a m i* pattern (ring, middle, index finger), practice a major scale on a single string at least five times in a row without pause. Have a metronome mark the first of every four notes:

Repeat this exercise on each string. When this entire sequence is perfect, increase the metronome speed by a notch and repeat the process. Continue until you achieve your maximum tempo without mistakes.

Another technique is to practice a tremolo piece very slowly, using a rest stroke only for the *m* finger. Increase the speed gradually with a metronome. When you can no longer use a rest stroke, use free strokes for all the fingers but continue to accent the middle finger. As the tempo increases, the accent will diminish, but the correct rhythmic placement should remain. Practice to your maximum tempo, keeping all the notes clear and even.

To maintain a clear articulation, use only the nail when striking with the *a*, *m*, and *i* fingers. And never bounce from the flesh to the nail—it will sound like a cat prancing on parquet.

What is the best way to damp a bass string when you don't want the sound to continue?

There are three basic ways to stop a ringing bass string: with the right-hand thumb; with a left-hand finger; and with the right-hand *i* (index), *m* (middle), or *a* (ring) fingers if one of them is playing rest stroke. A fourth alternative does exist when all else fails, but you need a relatively agile nose to try this one. In a recent recording session of the last Walton *Bagatelle,* I had no choice but to stop the low E with my nose, because my left-hand fingers were busy flying from the 13th to the 19th position, and I needed my thumb for an intense rest stroke on the fifth string. I don't recommend this method—strange harmonics often sound, the tip of your nose blackens after a few tries, and sneezing is common.

The first three techniques are clearly the most practical, and you can choose whichever is most comfortable and effective for a given situation. The most common approach is to use the right-hand thumb, but there is more than one way to do so. Although some people like to strike a new string and then return to silence the old one, this can be very awkward, both musically and technically. For example, if the low E of a dominant harmony is ringing and you wish to play the tonic harmony with a low A, the momentary dissonance that sounds while both strings ring is undesirable. If you are playing in a fast tempo, it may also be awkward to move the thumb back to E, or even impossible if it is needed somewhere else.

A far more effective technique is to stop the low E with the back of the thumb (just below the lower left corner of the cuticle) at the exact moment you touch the A with the nail and/or flesh. You can segue with either a perfectly smooth legato from E to A, or shorten the E, depending on the desired articulation. If you are moving in the opposite direction, say from A to E, you can silence the A by playing the E with a rest stroke thumb. Or if you desire a shorter articulation and there is time for a second motion, stop the A with your thumb before striking the E.

When you use a left-hand finger to stop an open string but do not continue with another pitch on that string, avoid landing on one of the loud natural harmonics (located over the fourth, fifth, seventh, ninth, and 12th frets). If you are stopping a fingered bass string with the left hand, lift your finger vertically to avoid unwanted glissandos or open string noises.

Finally, there may be situations where *i, m,* or *a* rest strokes are convenient for stopping an adjacent lower string. This approach will work, however, only when you desire a legato articulation between the two notes.

I find cross-string trills with *i, m,* and *a* to be musically fascinating but technically very difficult to play. Can you recommend any exercises?

Cross-string fingerings are most commonly used for Baroque ornaments that call for extra clarity and articulation, dynamic control, and/or lyricism (see Critical Notes and performance scores of Lute Suite BWV 996 and Lute Suite BWV 997 as edited by Rosalyn Tureck with fingering by Sharon Isbin, G. Schirmer; available through Guitar Solo Publications, 514 Bryant St., San Francisco, CA 94107). Cross-string trills, mordents, and turns use right-hand articulation on two or more strings rather than left-hand pull-off and hammer strokes on a single string.

A Baroque trill characteristically embellishes the main note from above:

If you play a trill moving from a lower string to a higher string, the right-hand fingering becomes *i m i a.*

Refining Techniques

A mordent starts on the main note, moves to its lower neighbor, and returns to the main note:

A turn is played as follows:

Because cross-string ornaments require such extraordinary dexterity and speed, it is essential to learn the technique first with exercises. I've developed three that work very effectively. Exercise 1 (see page 45) trains you to use four fingers on three strings. This is not as easy as it sounds, because we are used to playing arpeggios with four or more strings. Play the exercise with an even rhythm and work it up to your fastest possible speed with a metronome.

Using the same pattern of changing strings as in Exercise 1 (i.e., moving from playing the sixth, fifth, and fourth strings to playing the third, second, and first strings, and back again), play the following exercise with an even rhythm and work up to your maximum speed with a metronome.

Refining Techniques

Again using the same string pattern and approach as in Exercise 1, play the following exercise:

When you have mastered all the above, add a rhythmic variation to your routine by also playing the previous two exercises in short, fast bursts:

When sounding the last note of a cross-string embellishment, it is necessary to damp the previous note or notes in order to avoid harmonic confusion. You can accomplish this either by releasing a finger (or fingers when more than two strings are used) of the left hand or by damping the nonharmonic ringing with a right-hand finger. In the cross-string mordent below, the most effective way to stop the A is to release the second finger just after sounding the last B:

Refining Techniques

In other situations, it is more convenient to use a right-hand finger to stop the nonharmonic ringing. In the example below, which shows the basic right-hand trill pattern when going from a higher string to a lower string, use either the *m* or *a* finger to stop the final open E:

When the cross-string ornament is a mordent with an open string for the lower pitch, it is best to stop the nonharmonic ringing with the right-hand finger that would have played the next note had the ornament been a trill. The basic right-hand trill pattern when going from a lower string to a higher string is as follows:

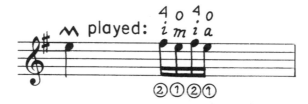

Therefore, use *a* to stop the open G in the mordent below:

With practice, cross-string damping eventually becomes second nature, and your fingers instinctively choose the most convenient and effective technique. Listen attentively at all times, and let your ear be the ultimate guide.

Refining Techniques

Exercise 1

What percussive techniques do you use in performance?

Tapping on the soundboard or bridge of the guitar is the most frequently used percussive technique. The guitar lends itself well to this effect because pitch and timbre vary throughout the instrument's body. Tonal Spanish composers, like Turina in his *Sevillana* and *Fandanguillo,* used it to recall the *golpe* of flamenco guitar. William Walton used tapping in his third *Bagatelle* for rhythmic color and emphasis. More recent composers use the technique to add new textures and coloristic effects. Leo Brouwer's *Canticum,* for instance, has passages that flutter improvisationally up and down the soundboard. His *Elogia de la Danza, El Decameron Negro,* and *Danza Caracteristica,* in contrast, all use tapping in a more rhythmic context.

Brouwer's *La Espiral Eterna* is the most adventurous of his percussive-style works. Here you'll find *pizzicato à la Bartók* (where the string is pulled up and snapped in its release), fingernails grating vertically across bass strings, and hammering with all ten fingers on the fingerboard. The effects are magical, especially in live performance. Other composers have employed spoons, bottlenecks, and other creative accoutrements to complement the sonic arsenal.

Even concertos use percussive effects. One of the most fascinating uses of tapping I've seen occurs in Lukas Foss' *American Landscapes.* In a beautiful slow-movement variation of "Wayfaring Stranger," the guitarist imitates the tune by tapping on three parts of the instrument while playing it at real pitch in canonic delay. John Corigliano's *Troubadours* concerto uses a snare drum–like technique, where the fifth and sixth strings are crossed by a left-hand finger and plucked with the right (a technique popularized by the Russian composer Nikita Koshkin). *Troubadours* also employs pitch-varied tapping and *pizzicato à la Bartók* to imitate tambourines and hand drums of 12th-century French dance bands.

Roadblocks

I have problems breathing while playing—shortness of breath, gasping, loud breathing. Can you recommend any solutions?

Breathing is the most tangible physical link we have between ourselves and the music. Musical and natural breathing can guide us along the slopes and contours of phrasing, melodic line, harmonic tension and resolution, and rhythmic intricacy. It allows the music to enter deeply within our bodies and to resonate with our own life force. Singers and wind and brass players are well aware of the need to nurture this relationship, for without breath they cannot even produce a sound. It is a constant challenge, because if they breathe improperly or in the wrong place, the phrasing, articulation, legato line, rhythm, intonation, and tone are often destroyed.

Guitarists, on the other hand, can ignore their breathing and still produce pitches, even if it means gasping or turning blue in the face. No matter what the instrument, however, one still needs to integrate breathing in order to play musically.

How can you accomplish this? First, study the music so that you have a clear knowledge of phrasing. Think of the beginning of each major phrase as a landmark where you will plan to inhale (either just before the phrase, before the upbeat, or with the upbeat figure, depending on the situation).

And don't forget to continue breathing within each phrase! Allow yourself to find that inner rhythm organically. Techniques like yoga and meditation can be useful in developing good breathing skills.

Some rests, tied notes, and syncopated rhythms can also serve as breathing landmarks. In the following example from measure 1 of J.S. Bach's Saraband, Suite BWV 996, inhale on the tied-over eighth note:

In measure 1 of Sor's Air #2, Op. 19, inhale on the eighth-note rest:

Roadblocks

There are also melodic and harmonic landmarks for breathing, but these are best demonstrated on the instrument.

Always remember to keep your chest, neck, throat, nostrils, mouth, tongue, and lips relaxed so that the air can flow freely. Breathe either through your mouth or nose, or both, whichever is most comfortable and quiet. Once you have connected your breathing to the music, you'll be amazed at how much more enjoyable it is to play and how much more expressive your music will be.

My teacher has told me to stop making faces when I play. How important is this?

If your facial gestures are genuine and natural expressions of mood and feeling, they can be an organic part of your performance. More often than not, however, facial grimaces are a product of tension and reflect awkward hand motions and strained technique. Such gestures only worsen overall tension and call attention to a player's discomfort. They can even fragment phrasing and impede legato playing since both require relaxed technique. When facial tension affects throat and ear muscles, breathing and hearing become constricted.

The visual impact of strange facial expressions is also terribly distracting for an audience. It's hard to take players seriously when their tongues are sticking out or they appear ready to sneeze at any moment! When in doubt, videotape your playing and see for yourself. The bottom line: if the image is not compatible with the music, it will detract from the performance. Practice with attention to relaxing your lips, jaw, tongue, eyebrows, ears, and neck. The natural emotive expressions will then emerge.

How do you determine the pitches of notes written high above the staff?

It can often be a bit daunting to decipher the innumerable lines and spaces above the staff that indicate the highest notes. Most guitars reach up to B, or sometimes even C, more than an octave above the first string when it is tuned to E.

To facilitate reading, uppermost pitches that occur in groups of four or more are sometimes written an octave lower and bracketed by *8va* above the notes to indicate their actual position. But when the written octave has not been changed and you are faced with a page that looks like a row of fire-engine ladders, there is an easy solution: If the note falls on a line, count five spaces downward from the adjacent upper space. The space you land on will be the desired pitch, an octave lower.

Similarly, when the note falls on a space, count five lines downward from the adjacent upper line.

My left hand becomes tired when I play full barre chords. How can I get a clear sound without a lot of finger pressure? Do you recommend any hand exercises or changes in the guitar's action?

Excessively high action will force your left hand to work harder than necessary. Adjust the bridge and nut to a level that just barely allows you to play loud rest strokes midway between the soundhole and bridge without buzzes.

Once the action is set, build your barring stamina gradually by practicing such pieces as Fernando Sor's Study #19 and Villa-Lobos' Etude #1. When barring, apply downward as well as perpendicular pressure, and roll the flesh upward, distributing it throughout the fret. Place your barring finger carefully so that the strings are not lodged in any joint crevices. Flatten the finger so that contact with the strings is solid. Always remember to use the least amount of pressure necessary to produce a clear sound.

Release the barre if you feel any pain or significant fatigue. It is better to stop and shake out your hand each time it becomes tired than to force your way prematurely through an entire piece. Your stamina and strength will gradually increase until fatigue is no longer a problem.

When either of my hands does feel tired after playing, I use a fabulous technique that Rosalyn Tureck shared with me some years ago. Run your hands under hot water for a few seconds (long enough for the heat to penetrate), then under cold water for a few seconds. Repeat about ten times, ending with the hot water. The expansion and contraction created by the alternating temperature extremes has a wonderfully relaxing effect on the muscles and may also serve to release toxins.

Roadblocks

I have just been through a prolonged period of numbness in my right hand during which I couldn't play the guitar. Now my hand is better, but atrophy seems to have set in. Do you know of any neat tricks or exercises I can use to limber up and strengthen my hand?

The safest way to regain your strength and dexterity is to practice on your instrument. However, since your muscles have lost much of their tone and stamina, work to regain your technique gradually. Sudden overuse could lead to new problems, such as tendinitis. If the fingertips of your left hand have lost their calluses, too many vigorous slurs could result in burst blood vessels. Practice arpeggio exercises, Villa-Lobos' Study #1, scales, slur exercises, and simple pieces. Return to more demanding repertoire only when your technique is up to the challenge.

If you wish to explore the possibility of supplemental hand exercises apart from those with the instrument, consult a reputable physical therapist who is affiliated with a hand doctor and who has experience working with musicians, including guitarists. The selection and application of such exercises should be based on the nature of the injury and on an analysis of the weakness and function of the muscles involved.

Finally, be sure that you have a clear understanding of how your numbness evolved in the first place. A faulty hand position; tension in the hand, arm, shoulder, neck, and/or back; a physical predisposition to carpal tunnel syndrome; and compressed nerves in the forearm can all lead to injury.

Few people realize how damaging the constant pressure of the forearm against the guitar's hard, sharp edge can be to delicate nerves. Those who aren't endowed with ample layers of fat or muscle padding are particularly vulnerable. If your forearm feels uncomfortable, you may have an unconscious tendency to lift your arm ever so slightly, causing tension throughout. An even more serious consequence would be nerve damage. You can avoid both problems by resting the arm on a bit of padding. What I use is a washcloth folded into a thickness of about five layers. I either attach it to the outside of my sleeve with Velcro or wear on my arm a cylindrical cloth with a pouch that holds the pad. If you wear the pad on the outside, match its color with the sleeve of your performance garment. You can also create removable slipcovers for different outfits.

Where Mind Meets Music

I'm having difficulty memorizing. Should I try to memorize the musical score or the finger patterns on the fretboard, or should I think in terms of chords?

The more you understand the language and structure of a piece, the easier it will be to memorize. The same is true with any form of learning that involves complex thought patterns. We've all had the experience at one time or another, for example, of trying to memorize poetry or lines from a play. The ease or difficulty of that process is determined by one's understanding of the emotional, historical, personal, and structural context of what an author is expressing. If you perceive the text as merely unrelated individual words or sentences, or as unintelligible sounds (as in a foreign language), the brain has little incentive to retain it. However, if you understand the words and integrate them within a logical pattern of thought, memorizing becomes much easier.

Similarly, one's ability to remember a musical score is enhanced by a clear understanding of the phrasing and the melodic, rhythmic, and harmonic structure of the work. Before learning a piece, write out phrasing marks so that the structural units are clear. Indicate both small and large units of phrasing, and outline the large structure as well. Identify important harmonic landmarks and modulations. Add right- and left-hand fingerings that best express the phrasing, voicing, counterpoint, desired articulation, and chosen timbre. Then practice the music phrase by phrase and section by section.

As an example, play the line on page 51, from the Prelude to J.S. Bach's Suite BWV 996 [edited by Rosalyn Tureck, fingering by Sharon Isbin, published by G. Schirmer]. Repeat each larger phrase (indicated by the letters A, B, C, etc.) until you memorize it. Then join the phrases together one by one.

Practice the remaining lines of the Passaggio section of the Prelude in this manner. When you can play it by heart, put away the guitar and visualize the left-hand (and eventually the right-hand) finger patterns, section by section. If you have trouble playing without the score before you've done the mental work, then introduce visualization earlier, alternating it with repeated playings of each phrase. When a finger or fret is not clear, refer to the score. I prefer to visualize the fingers, frets, and strings rather than actual notes, because these are the final images sent by the brain before a sound is produced.

This combined method of analysis, motor repetition, and visualization increases not only the speed of memorization but also its solidity and staying power.

Where Mind Meets Music

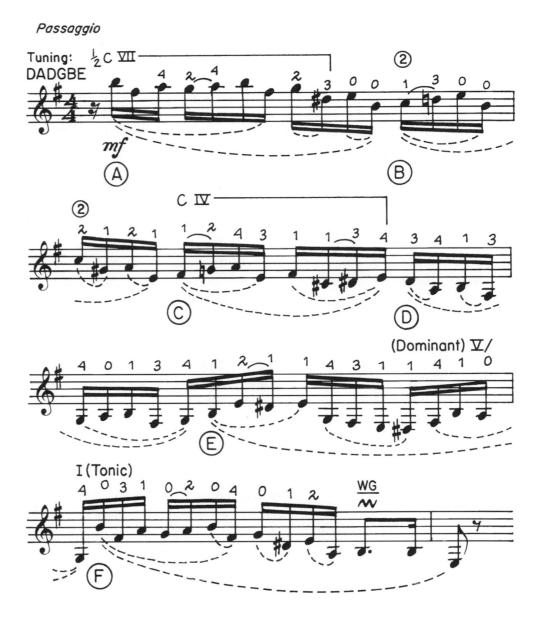

Passaggio

How do you relax and concentrate before and during a performance? Sometimes I become tense and nervous on stage, and my playing suffers.

In order to be relaxed and confident, it is essential to be well prepared long before the concert. Learn the music fluently and conscientiously as much in advance as possible. Once you have learned a piece, rehearse it from start to finish to explore the full range of musical expression and to develop the requisite physical and mental stamina. You may still need to isolate sections to address specific technical challenges.

Strengthen memory and concentration skills by practicing each of the pieces mentally, without the instrument. To do this, visualize all the left-hand (and eventually all the right-hand) fingering patterns while you hear the music in your mind exactly as you wish it to sound. At first, have the score handy to correct and rehearse any sections that are not clear; you may also have to work fast passages up to tempo gradually. Pace yourself so that you can visualize the entire program flawlessly, without the aid of scores, at least ten days before the concert. During the week prior to the concert, continue to rehearse the program with this visualization technique each day. This approach, because it is unhampered by the technical difficulties of an instrument, also allows you to develop and expand your musical goals and vision.

When you feel confident with each piece, practice playing through the entire program. You should do this daily at least ten days before a concert to develop stamina. Work on individual pieces additionally when necessary. And it is an invaluable experience to play through your program informally for others.

It is also helpful to practice some form of relaxation or meditation on a regular basis. I have done transcendental meditation since age 17, and it has been a wonderful way for me to reduce stress, reinforce memory and concentration, and expand musical expression. On the day of a concert, I follow my daily routine of meditating once in the morning for 20 minutes and then again in the afternoon. You can also introduce positive suggestions while in this trancelike state, because the mind is especially receptive. As in autohypnosis, however, only suggest ideas that are believable and realistic, and don't drill. Replacing negative thoughts about performance with positive ones can be as simple as reprogramming a computer. There is no reason to allow irrational demons—conscious or subconscious—to dominate your thinking or undermine your self-confidence.

If you have prepared effectively, there is little more to do the day of a concert than warm up with a few scales and exercises and run through the program very softly, saving your energy for the performance. You might also wish to play fast passages under tempo. Rest and relax after practicing, have a good meal about three hours before, and warm up again just before the performance. Then go for it!

If you have effectively prepared for a performance but still feel tense on stage, you might consider the question of musical and spiritual immersion. Are you really *listening* to the music you play? For the more you are engaged musically, the less time you will have to be nervous or distracted. Are you actively *feeling* the music, emotionally and spiritually? If not, your subconscious could be saying, "This whole process is a big lie, and I don't really care what happens."

After all, you have to believe in what you are doing in order to be effective, and that is possible only when you are giving it your heart and soul. You must be able to identify with and feel the music you are playing. And remember to emote in the practice room, because that is what allows your feelings to be free and open on stage.

If the issue for you is not musical or emotional, then perhaps it is psychological. One can have the best intentions and make excellent preparations but still suffer from irrational fears that block the flow of positive energy. Sometimes these fears were once

Where Mind Meets Music

realistic and legitimate and have carried over from earlier days when you didn't really know how to prepare effectively. With effort and determination, you can deprogram these gremlins and replace them with positive, believable thoughts. Self-hypnosis and repetitive writing can be helpful in this quest to be more in control of your conscious and subconscious patterns of thinking.

How should I practice so that I don't trip over single mistakes in a performance? I tend to memorize pieces in phrases, not by remembering notes but by visualizing the position and motion of the left hand. Hence, when I miss a note, I miss the phrase, and the whole song is interrupted.

It seems that you are immersing yourself in individual fragments without getting the big picture. Mentally coordinate the visualization of your left-hand fingers with the sound of the notes, hear the notes within the context of a phrase, and study the relationship of individual phrases to each other and to the rhythmic, melodic, and harmonic structure of the entire piece. In addition to learning individual details of a work, you must unite and integrate them into a continuum of thought that has direction and purpose.

If you form a large frame of reference built solidly on structural components, a single glitch won't derail you, because you'll know exactly where the piece is heading.

Making a Career

I am composing music for classical guitar. Who publishes this kind of music, and how should I approach them?

A publisher will take an unsolicited manuscript more seriously if the score is neatly copied (preferably typeset on a computer) and accompanied by letters of recommendation from respected guitarists, a professional resumé, and an excellent quality recording. If a guitarist who champions your work already has a relationship with a publisher, it may be more effective for her or him to make the initial approach on your behalf. Most publishers will only be interested in works that they can expect to sell—so if you can't interest performers in the music, it won't seem marketable to a publisher.

How do you interest performers? Musical America publishes an annual *International Directory of the Performing Arts* in which classical performers with management in the United States are listed by instrument. It's always a long shot, but you can try sending scores (and tapes) to guitarists in care of their managers and hope that someone will take the time to look at them. It would be unrealistic to *expect* an answer, however, since your inquiry is unsolicited. If the work is wonderful, it will sell itself. If you don't get an answer, assume the individual is not interested and try someone else. If you never get any positive response from performers, show your piece to a respected composition teacher for musical advice and guidance.

If you are fortunate enough to summon up the requisite artistic backing, there are many companies you could approach who currently publish guitar music. Order a catalogue from Guitar Solo (514 Bryant St., San Francisco, CA 94107), which includes listings that will give you an excellent idea of who publishes what. For starters, here are some names that come to mind: Guitar Solo Publications, Orphée, G. Schirmer, Music Sales, Boosey and Hawkes, European American, Peer-Southern, Mel Bay, Theodore Presser, Hal Leonard, MMB Music, American Composers Alliance, Cavata Music Publishers, Editions Salabert, Schott and Co., Chanterelle, Zanibon, Brazilliance, Suvini Zerboni, Novello, Faber, UME, Max Eschig, Tecla, Edizioni Musicali Bèrben, Carl Fischer, Sikorski, Ricordi, and Editions Musicales Transatlantiques. Addresses for most of these companies are listed in the Musical America *International Directory of the Performing Arts.*

How can a classical guitarist—one among so many—find a niche and make a living by performing and teaching?

There are never any guarantees. But if you want to teach, you should get a master's or doctorate degree in music from a reputable university or conservatory. It might be useful to become proficient in other areas of music as well—such as theory, history, ear training, jazz or folk styles—since job descriptions often involve skills in addition to teaching classical guitar. And it is essential to have excellent training before the graduate level. Ideally a player should be well versed, technically and stylistically, in the different periods of music from the Renaissance to contemporary.

For the aspiring performer, the most important question to ask is, What can I contribute to the guitar world that will be different, valuable, and compelling? To answer

Making a Career

this requires searching one's innermost resources to discover and create something extraordinary that has never been done before. It may mean bringing unusual repertoire to the fore by unearthing and editing lost or forgotten compositions, or by making innovative, effective transcriptions and arrangements. Working with outstanding composers to create new works also has great potential. The collaboration could expand the musical vision and technical resources of the guitar, increase the instrument's exposure, and further enhance its credibility, especially when prestigious composers are involved.

Other ideas to pursue might include performing in unusual ensembles, creating new fusion approaches, and developing technical innovations. Above all, the player should aspire to musicality of the highest order, technical control and fluency, and a strong, personal, and distinctive voice.

Notes on Concert Programming

Knowing how to design an effective concert program is an important part of performing. One must find that magical combination of works that succeeds in captivating the audience from the start, maintaining their interest throughout the performance, and ending with a climax that leaves them wanting more.

Length is important: 32–40 minutes of music in each half of the program is a good guideline. Once you factor in applause, talk, and encores, it's a full evening. Choose music of quality—nothing kills a program faster than B-rate music or works that are ill suited to your personality and skills. Start with a work that will immediately engage both you and your audience, something you enjoy playing and feel completely confident performing under pressure. When ordering pieces, vary the tempo so that the program doesn't become static. Select something strong to precede the intermission so that the audience is eager to return. Since audiences are particularly alert just after the intermission, that is a good time to play something especially challenging to the listener (note the position of *Clocks* in the program on page 58). Build to a powerful ending, one that's exciting in terms of virtuosity and/or powerful from an emotional perspective.

How do you choose the repertoire? Should there be a theme? You can program thematically by style, composer, era, form, format, or subject. For example, the program could focus on a single composer (see the all-Bach 300th anniversary program on page 59), or you could dedicate a performance to a particular composer and include related works (see García Lorca 100th anniversary program, page 64). The evening could focus on a particular era, such as the 20th century or the Romantic period. The voice and guitar program I do with Susanne Mentzer, for instance (see page 62), is centered around folk-inspired music in both the duets and the solos and is modeled after our recording, *Wayfaring Stranger*.

Another thematic approach would be to highlight one particular culture or place, such as Spain, Latin America, Italy, or America. I tend not to go in that direction too often because I prefer more variety. For example, when performing with Thiago de Mello, I combine South American repertoire from our *Journey to the Amazon* CD with Spanish solos. It's still thematic but in a more inclusive way (see page 65).

That said, you'll notice three programs here (on pages 58, 60, and 61) that have no particular thematic concept. However, they are composed of repertoire that works well together and provides contrast, depth, and variety. Chronological ordering of works is not necessary and in fact would have been detrimental to these programs.

When determining a program, you may find it helpful to write down the works and their timings on individual note cards. Position them on a table and try different combinations until you find the winning one.

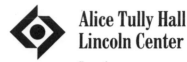

**Alice Tully Hall
Lincoln Center**

Home of
The Chamber Music Society
of Lincoln Center

Sunday Afternoon, November 25, 1990, at 3:00

GREAT PERFORMERS AT LINCOLN CENTER
Underwritten by Continental Insurance
presents

SHARON ISBIN
Guitar

LEO BROUWER	The Black Decameron (1981) *(Written for Sharon Isbin)* Lovers Fleeing Through the Valley of the Echoes Harp of the Warrior The Maiden in Love
	La espiral eterna (1971)
J. S. BACH	Suite, BWV 997 Edited by Rosalyn Tureck/ Fingering by S. Isbin; Published by G. Schirmer, Inc. Prelude Fugue Sarabande Gigue Double

Intermission

JOAN TOWER	Clocks (1985) *(New York Premiere—Written for Sharon Isbin)*
WILLIAM WALTON	Five Bagatelles (1971) Allegro Lento, Tempo di valse Alla Cubana Sempre espressivo Con stancio
JOAQUIN RODRIGO	Invocación y Danza
AGUSTIN BARRIOS	vvaltz, Op. 8, No. 4
	La catedral Andante religioso Allegro solemne
ANTONIO LAURO	Venezuelan Waltz No. 3 ("Valse Criollo")
	Seis por derecho

ORCHESTRA OF SANTA FE

BACH FESTIVAL

FESTIVAL RECITAL

Thursday, January 31, 1985 / 8 p.m. / St. Francis Auditorium

SHARON ISBIN, Guitar

PROGRAM

Lute Suite in E minor, BWV 996   *JOHANN SEBASTIAN BACH*
   (Edited by Rosalyn Tureck/Fingering by Ms. Isbin)   *(1685-1750)*

   Prelude
   Allemande
   Courante
   Sarabande
   Bourée
   Gigue

Lute Suite in C minor, BWV 997   *JOHANN SEBASTIAN BACH*

   (Edited by Rosalyn Tureck/Fingering by Ms. Isbin/Transcribed to A minor by Rosalyn Tureck)

   Prelude
   Fugue
   Sarabande
   Gigue
   Double

INTERMISSION

Two Preludes   *JOHANN SEBASTIAN BACH*

Lute Suite in E major, BWV 1006a   *JOHANN SEBASTIAN BACH*
   (Edited by Rosalyn Tureck/Fingering by Ms. Isbin)

   Prelude
   Loure
   Gavotte en Rondeau
   Minuet I
   Minuet II
   Bourée
   Gigue

WIGMORE HALL

Wigmore Street, London W1
Manager : William Lyne

Friday, 20th May, 1977

at 7.30 p.m.

SHARON ISBIN

guitar

PROGRAMME

Canticum : I Eclosion	LEO BROUWER
II Ditirambo	b. 1939
Danza Caracteristica	
La Espiral Eterna	
Lute Suite No. 3	J. S. BACH
Prelude	1685-1750
Allemande	
Courante	
Sarabande	
Gavotte I and II	
Gigue	

INTERMISSION

Sonata Eroica	MAURO GIULIANI
	1781-1840
Mallorca	ISAAC ALBENIZ
	1860-1909
Partita for Guitar	STEPHEN DODGSON
Allegretto con moto	b. 1924
Molto vivace	
Adagio	
Allegro	
Three Venezuelan Waltzes	ANTONIO LAURO
	b. 1917

Alice Tully Hall

Lincoln Center for the Performing Arts

Thursday Evening, March 29, 1979 at 8:00

GEORGE COCHRAN
presents

The New York Recital Debut of

SHARON ISBIN

Guitarist

LEO BROUWER	Canticum Eclosíon Ditirambo Danza Característica
ENRIQUE GRANADOS	Danza Española No. 5
NICCOLO PAGANINI	Romanza (from Grand Sonata)

BENJAMIN BRITTEN	Nocturnal (after John Dowland, Opus 70)
	Musingly, very Agitated,
	  Restless, Uneasy, March–like
	Dreaming, Gently rocking,
	  Passacaglia, Theme

Intermission

J.S. BACH	Lute Suite No. 1 (transcribed and edited by Rosalyn Tureck; fingered by Sharon Isbin) Prelude Allemande Courante Sarabande Bourrée Gigue
BRUCE MacCOMBIE	Nightshade Rounds (World Premiere)
ISAAC ALBENIZ	Mallorca Sevilla

This concert is made possible, in part, by grants from the Jerome Foundation, Inc. of Minneapolis, the Schubert Club of Minnesota, and the Martha Baird Rockefeller Foundation.

A George Cochran Production
330 West 58th Street
Suite 218
New York, New York 10019
(212) 582-1222

Theresa L. Kaufmann Concert Hall
Tuesday, February 9, 1999

The Guitar: From Bach to Bossa Nova
Sharon Isbin, Artistic Director

Sharon Isbin, guitar
Susanne Mentzer, mezzo-soprano

Franz Schubert   Three Lieder

         Ständchen (Transcribed by Sharon Isbin)
         Heidenröslein
         Nachtstück

Traditional   Four Bergerettes (18th Century French Folksongs)
Arranged by Siegfied Behrend/Revised by Sharon Isbin

         Jeunes Fillettes
         Que ne suis-je la fougère!
         L'amour s'envole
         Maman, dites-moi

Susanne Mentzer and Sharon Isbin

Francisco Tárrega   Capricho Arabe

Sharon Isbin

Traditional   Four French Folk Songs - Arranged by Matyas Seiber

         Réveillez-vous
         J'ai descendu
         Le Rossignol
         Marguerite, elle est malade

Susanne Mentzer and Sharon Isbin

Intermission

John Duarte	Appalachian Dreams, Op. 121 (*premiere*)
	(*written for Sharon Isbin - commissioned with funds from*
	the Augustine Foundation)

      I.   Fantasia: Katy cruel - Shady grove - The foggy, foggy dew
      II. Black is the color of my true love's hair
      III. Darling Cora
      IV. Putney Hymn
      V. Finale: O'Brien's Jig - Red-haired boy -
          Planxty George Brabazon

Sharon Isbin

| Traditional | Five American Folk Songs |

Black is the color of my true love's hair
(Arr. Laurindo Almeida)
Red Rosey Bush (Arr. Carlos Barbos-Lima)
Go 'way from my window (John Jacob Niles, Trans. S. Isbin)
The Nightingale (Arr. Barbosa-Lima)
Wayfaring Stranger (Arr. Barbosa-Lima)

Susanne Mentzer and Sharon Isbin

This series is sponsored, in part, by
Albert Augustine, Ltd., maker of guitar strings.

"AUGUSTINE" STRINGS

The taking of photographs and the use of recording equipment are not allowed in the concert hall.
Please make sure the electronic signal on your watch or pager is turned off before the concert begins.

Theresa L. Kaufmann Concert Hall
Sunday, April 5, 1998 at 3 p.m.

The 92nd Street Y Tisch Center for the Arts
and
Metropolitan Life Foundation
present

Sharon Isbin, guitar
with guest artists
Denyce Graves, mezzo-soprano
Ana Maria Martinez, soprano

Readers: **Angel González** and **Christopher Maurer**

100th Anniversary Tribute to Federico García Lorca (1898-1936)

Enrique Granados	Spanish Dance No. 5
Francisco Tárrega	Capricho Arabe
	Recuerdos de la Alhambra

Ms. Isbin

Reading: Federico García Lorca: *Adivinanza de la Guitarra (Riddle of the Guitar)*

Joaquin Turina	Fandanguillo
Regino Sainz de la Maza	Zapateado

Ms. Isbin

Manuel de Falla	Siete Canciones Populares Españolas (arr. M. Llobet/E. Pujol)
	El paño moruno, Seguidilla murciana, Asturiana, Nana, Canción, Polo

Ms. Graves and Ms. Isbin

Intermission

Joaquin Rodrigo	Aranjuez, Ma Pensée (Adagio from Concierto de Aranjuez)

Ms. Graves and Ms. Isbin

Reading: Federico García Lorca: *La Guitarra (The Guitar)*

Federico García Lorca	5 Canciones Españolas Antiguas (arr. Sharon Isbin)
	Anda, Jaleo
	Las Morillas de Jaén
	El Café de Chinitas
	Nana de Sevilla
	Sevillanas del Siglo XVIII

Ms. Martinez and Ms. Isbin

Reading: Federico García Lorca: *Las Seis Cuerdas (The Six Strings); Memento (Memento)*

Isaac Albeniz	Mallorca (arr. Andrès Segovia)
	Asturias

Ms. Isbin

The taking of photographs and the use of recording equipment are not allowed in the concert hall.
Please make sure the electronic signal on your watch or pager is turned off before the concert begins.

SAN FRANCISCO PERFORMANCES

in association with Omni Foundation for the Performing Arts

PRESENTS

SHARON ISBIN, guitar

Gaudencio Thiago de Mello, Brazilian percussion

Friday, January 10, 1997, 8:00 p.m., Herbst Theatre

I

ENRIQUE GRANADOS/*arr. Michael Llobet*	Spanish Dance No. 5
ISAAC ALBÉNIZ/*arr. Andrés Segovia*	Asturias
FRANCISCO TÁRREGA	Recuerdos de la Alhambra
GAUDENCIO THIAGO DE MELLO	Lago de Janaucà

Sharon Isbin

II

GAUDENCIO THIAGO DE MELLO	Four Chants for the Chief
	A chamada dos ventos / Cançao Noturna
	Uirapuru do Amazonas
	Cunhã-tan do Andirá
	Varando Furos

Sharon Isbin & Gaudencio Thiago de Mello

INTERMISSION

III

LEO BROUWER	Cançion de Cuna
ALFREDO VIANNA (PIXINGUINHA)	Vou vivendo
VIANNA/*arr. Carlos Barbosa-Lima*	Cochichando
THIAGO DE MELLO	Chôro alegre
THIAGO DE MELLO	Abraço no Pixinga

Sharon Isbin & Gaudencio Thiago de Mello

IV

HEITOR VILLA-LOBOS	Etudes No. 8 & 11

Sharon Isbin

V

GENTIL MONTAÑA	Porro
BENITO CANONICO/*arr. Lauro/Diaz*	Aire de Jorope
ANTONIO LAURO	Waltz No. 3
ANTONIO LAURO	Seis por derecho

Sharon Isbin & Gaudencio Thiago de Mello

Sharon Isbin is represented by Columbia Artists Management, Inc., New York
EMI/Virgin Classics and Concord Records

 Sharon Isbin and Gaudencio Thiago de Mello are generously donating a portion of their fee for tonight's concert, which San Francisco Performances is matching, as a contribution to Classical Action: Performing Arts Against AIDS.

Guitar Player Magazine is the print media sponsor of the 1996-97 Guitar Series

Please show consideration for the artists and other patrons by making sure that your digital watch alarm or beeper is switched **off** before the performance begins.

The John F. Kennedy Center for the Performing Arts

RALPH P. DAVIDSON, *Chairman*
MARTA ISTOMIN, *Artistic Director*

CONCERT HALL
Friday Evening, March 31, 1989, at 8:30

HUGH H. SMITH,
President
DOUGLAS H. WHEELER,
Managing Director
PATRICK HAYES,
Managing Director Emeritus

presents

Guitarjam

SHARON ISBIN, *guitar*
LARRY CORYELL, *guitar*
LAURINDO ALMEIDA, *guitar*

Program may include the following:

MANUEL DE FALLA arr. Ian Krouse	Miller's Dance
RADAMES GNATTALI arr. Laurindo Almeida	Ballade Samba
GNATTALI arr. Almeida	Baion

Trio

ENRIQUE MADRIGUERA arr. Almeida	Adiós
ALFREDO VIANNA (PIXINGUINHA) arr. Almeida	Cochichando

Sharon Isbin and Laurindo Almeida

To Be Announced
Sharon Isbin

FALLA   Popular Spanish Songs
El paño moruno
Jota
Polo
Sharon Isbin and Larry Coryell

To Be Announced
Larry Coryell

LAURINDO ALMEIDA	Brazilliance
LARRY CORYELL	P.S.P. No. 2

Trio

Intermission

The taking of photographs and the use of recording equipment are not allowed in this auditorium.
The Filene Memorial Organ in the Concert Hall contributed by Mrs. Jouett Shouse.
Baldwin is the official piano and electronic organ of the Kennedy Center.

CLAUDE DEBUSSY "Clair de lune" Samba
arr. Almeida
Laurindo Almeida

ANTONIO CARLOS JOBIM How Insensitive
Laurindo Almeida and **Larry Coryell**

GNATTALI Chiquinha Gonzaga
arr. Almeida

JOAQUÍN RODRIGO Adagio, from "Concierto
arr. Almeida de Aranjuez"

CORYELL P.S.P. No. 1
Trio

Artists will announce selections from the stage.

The Washington Performing Arts Society is grateful to Pacific Telesis Foundation for taking a leadership role in support of the WPAS Family Initiative Program.

In addition, we wish to thank Ameritech Foundation, Anonymous,
The April Trust, AT&T, Clark-Winchcole Foundation, Dimick Foundation,
John Edward Fowler Memorial Foundation, Philip L. Graham Fund, and the
Eugene and Agnes E. Meyer Foundation for their support.

Courtesy car compliments of **Moore Cadillac Company**

Concerti for Guitar and Orchestra
Performed by Sharon Isbin

Laurindo Almeida, *Amazonia,* Brazilliance Music Publishing, scored for strings and percussion, 6 minutes.

Laurindo Almeida, *Lobiana,* Brazilliance Music Publishing, scored for strings, 8 minutes.

Lennox Berkeley, Guitar Concerto, Opus 88, Chester Music, scored for flute, oboe, clarinet in B♭, bassoon, two horns in F, and strings, 22 minutes. Written for Julian Bream and premiered in London, July 4, 1974.

Leo Brouwer, *Concierto Elegiaco,* Editions Max Eschig, scored for strings and percussion, 24 minutes. Written for Julian Bream and premiered in London, July 30, 1986. Premiered by Isbin in Finland, June 30, 1987; in France, March 13, l988; and in the USA (New York's Town Hall), November 9, 1988.

Leo Brouwer, *Tres Danzas Concertantes,* Editions Max Eschig, scored for strings, 15 minutes.

Ferdinando Carulli, Concerto in G Major for Flute, Guitar, and Orchestra, Suvini Serboni, scored for strings, two oboes, and two horns, 17 minutes.

John Corigliano, *Troubadours for Guitar and Orchestra,* G. Schirmer, scored for two flutes (piccolo), two oboes (English horn), two clarinets in A and B♭, two bassoons, two horns in F, percussion, piano (optional), and strings, 23 minutes. Written for Isbin and premiered with the St. Paul Chamber Orchestra and conductor Hugh Wolff at the Ordway Music Theatre, St. Paul, Minnesota, October 8, 1993.

Tan Dun, *Yi 2: Concerto for Guitar and Orchestra,* G. Schirmer, scored for two flutes (piccolo), two oboes, clarinet in B♭, bass clarinet, bassoon, contrabassoon, two horns in F, two trumpets in B♭, two trombones, percussion (four players), piano, harp, and strings, 32 minutes. Written for Isbin and premiered with the Orchestre National de France at the Donaueschingen Festival, Germany, October 18, 1996. Premiered in the U.K. with the BBC Scottish Symphony and conductor Tan Dun, Glasgow, Scotland, November 28, 1996.

Lukas Foss, *American Landscapes,* Carl Fischer, scored for flute, oboe, clarinet, bassoon, trumpet, horn, trombone, percussion, piano, harp, and strings, 27 minutes. Written for Isbin and premiered with the Orchestra of St. Luke's and conductor Lukas Foss, Avery Fisher Hall, New York, New York, November 29, 1989.

George Gershwin, *Rhapsody in Blue,* arranged by Carlos Barbosa-Lima for two guitars and orchestra, oboe, clarinet (B♭ and bass), flute, alto sax (optional), two horns in F, trumpet in B♭, two trombones, timpani, and strings, 17 minutes. Isbin and Barbosa-Lima performed the world premiere of this arrangement at the Waterville Valley Festival, New Hampshire, July 15, 1989.

Mauro Giuliani, Concerto in A Major, Opus 30, Suvini Zerboni, scored for strings only or two flutes, two oboes, two clarinets, two bassoons, two horns, and strings, 20 minutes.

Aaron Jay Kernis, Double Concerto for Guitar and Violin, G. Schirmer, scored for two flutes (piccolo), two oboes (English horn), two clarinets in B♭ (A and bass clarinet), two bassoons (contrabassoon), two horns in F, two trumpets in C, percussion (three players), harp, celesta (synthesizer and upright), and strings, 31 minutes. Written for Isbin and premiered by Isbin and Nadja Salerno-Sonnenberg with the St. Paul Chamber Orchestra and conductor Hugh Wolff, Minneapolis, Minnesota, February 6, 1997.

Ami Maayani, Concerto for Guitar and Orchestra, Lyra Music Co., scored for full orchestra, 24 minutes. Written for Isbin and premiered with the Minnesota Orchestra, Orchestra Hall, Minneapolis, Minnesota, April 1978. Isbin's first commissioned work and premiere.

Bruce MacCombie, *Nightshade Rounds,* European American, scored for strings, 11 minutes. Written for Isbin and premiered with the Brooklyn Philharmonic and conductor Lukas Foss, Cooper Union Hall, New York, New York, March 18, 1988. Originally written as a guitar solo.

Manuel Ponce, *Concierto del Sur,* Peer International, scored for chamber orchestra, 23 minutes. Written for Andrés Segovia.

Joaquín Rodrigo, *Concierto de Aranjuez,* European American, scored for two flutes (piccolo), two oboes (English horn), two clarinets in B♭, two bassoons, two horns in F, two trumpets in C, and strings, 24 minutes. Written for Regino Sainz de la Maza, who premiered it in Barcelona, Spain, November 9, 1940.

Joaquín Rodrigo, *Fantasia para un Gentilhombre,* European American, scored for flute (piccolo), oboe, bassoon, trumpet in C, and strings, 23 minutes. Written for Segovia and premiered in San Francisco, California, March 5, 1958.

Christopher Rouse, *Concert de Gaudí,* Boosey and Hawkes, 25 minutes. Written for Isbin for premiere with the NDR Symphony and conductor Christoph Eschenbach, Hamburg, Germany, January 2, 2000.

Joseph Schwantner, *From Afar . . . A Fantasy for Guitar and Orchestra,* European American, scored for chamber orchestra or full orchestra: piccolo, two flutes, two oboes, English horn, two B♭ clarinets, bass clarinet, two bassoons, contrabassoon, four horns, three trumpets in C, three trombones, tuba, piano/celesta, harp, percussion (three players), timpani, and strings, 15 minutes. Written for Isbin and premiered with the St. Louis Symphony and conductor Leonard Slatkin, St. Louis, Missouri, January 8, 1988; and Carnegie Hall, New York, New York, January 30, 1988.

Ivana Themmen, Concerto for Guitar and Orchestra, Lyra Music Corp., scored for full orchestra, 23 minutes. Written for Isbin and premiered with the Minnesota Orchestra, Orchestra Hall, Minneapolis, Minnesota, November 1981.

Heitor Villa-Lobos, Concerto for Guitar and Small Orchestra, Editions Max Eschig, scored for flute, oboe, clarinet in B♭, bassoon, horn in F, trombone, and strings, 18 minutes. Written for Segovia in 1951.

Antonio Vivaldi, Concerto in A Major, scored for strings, 12 minutes.

Antonio Vivaldi, Concerto in C Major, scored for strings, 12 minutes.

Antonio Vivaldi, Concerto in D Major, scored for strings, 12 minutes.

Nylon-String Guitar Makers

This listing of nylon-string guitar makers was compiled from the membership list of the Association of Stringed Instrument Artisans (see the listings for ASIA and the other American association for guitar makers, the Guild of American Luthiers, on page 76). We also received help from Beverly Maher at the Guitar Salon in New York (see the listing of salons and shops specializing in classical guitars on page 75). A comprehensive, searchable directory of makers and manufacturers can be found on *Acoustic Guitar*'s Web site, www.acousticguitar.com.

United States

Carl Barney Guitars
PO Box 128
Southbury, CT 06488
(203) 264-9207

Bob Beckwith
50 Voyagers Lane
Ashland, MA 01721
(508) 881-3648

David Berkowitz
251 12th St. S.E.
Washington, DC 20003
(202) 546-0236
www.berkowitzguitars.com

Gordon Bischoff Guitars
5150 Deerfield Rd.
Eau Claire, WI 54701
(715) 832-8915

Rob Bishline
202 S. 193rd East Ave. #25
Tulsa, OK 74108
(918) 835-6959

Julius Borges III
694 Great Rd.
Littleton, MA 01460
(508) 358-0358

Mark Brumitt
103 Coronado Ave.
St. Augustine, FL 32084
(904) 825-0482

Brian Burns
615 Middlefield Rd.
Palo Alto, CA 94301
(415) 327-5335

Steve Cain
851 Congress St., Apt. 1
Portland, ME 04102
(616) 592-0905

David Cassotta
5000 Plumbago Pl.
Rocklin, CA 95677
(614) 624-3794

William Cumpiano
237B South St.
Northampton, MA 01060-4111
(413) 586-3730
eljibaro@crocker.com
members.tripod.com/
~cumpiano

John Curttright
12444 Rockton Ave.
Rockton, IL 61072
(815) 624-4770

J. Thomas Davis
3135 N. High St.
Columbus, OH 43202
(614) 263-0264
Fax (614) 447-0174
JTDGuitars@aol.com

Lester DeVoe
Long Look Farm
668 Paris Hill Rd.
South Paris, ME 04281
(207) 743-9764
mainlyus@megalink.net
www.maui.net/~rtadaki/
devoe.html

Maurice Dupont Guitars
2550 Smith Grade
Santa Cruz, CA 95060
(831) 427-0343
Fax (831) 427-0343
Music@cruzio.com

Gila Eban
PO Box 95
Riverside, CT 06878
(203) 625-8307

Jeffrey Elliott
2812 S. E. 37th Ave.
Portland, OR 97202
(503) 233-0836

Mark Erlewine
4402 Burnet Rd. #B
Austin, TX 78756
(512) 302-1225
Fax (512) 371-1655

Everett Guitar Works
2338 Johnson Ferry
Atlanta, GA 30341
(770) 451-2485
everett@mindspring.com

Ronald Fernández
PO Box 5153
Irvine, CA 92616
(714) 856-1529

Larry Fitzgerald
2 Flax Lane
Levittown, NY 11756
(516) 731-8354

Fleishman Instruments
4500 Whitney Pl.
Boulder, CO 80303
(303) 499-1614
guitars@henge.com
www.henge.com/~guitars

Gallagher Guitars
PO Box 128
Wartrace, TN 37183
(615) 389-6455
dong@cafes.net
www.dnj.com/gallagher

Gilbert Guitars
1485 La Honda Rd.
Woodside, CA 94062
(415) 851-1239
Fax (415) 851-3284

Hill Guitar Co.
PO Box 986
Ben Lomond, CA 95005
(408) 336-2436
Fax (408) 336-2436
khill@hillguitar.com
www.hillguitar.com

Charles A. Hoffman Guitars
2219 E. Franklin Ave.
Minneapolis, MN 55404
(612) 338-1079

Tom Humphrey
1167 Bruynswick Rd.
Gardiner, NY 12525
(212) 696-1693
HUMPHgtr@aol.com

Stephen Janofsky
493 West Pelham Rd.
Amherst, MA 01002
(413) 259-1072

David Johnson
PO Box 222
Talkeetna, AK 99676
(907) 733-2777

Dee Jones
Thunder Lion Guitars
1515 Upland Dr.
Silver Spring, MD 20905
(301) 421-1816

Glen Jordan
407 Kearney St.
El Cerrito, CA 94530
(510) 528-3614

John Jordan
1173 Linden Dr.
Concord, CA 94520
(510) 671-9246

Daniel Knowles
616 N. Market St.
Paris, TN 38242
(901) 644-1157

K & S Music
2923 Adeline St.
Berkeley, CA 94703-2502
(510) 644-1958
Fax (510) 644-1958
kands@california.com
www.california.com/~kands

Peter Langdell
RR 2, Box 5810
Junction Hill
Jeffersonville, VT 05464
(802) 644-2233

Augustino LoPrinzi
1929 Drew St.
Clearwater FL 33765
(813) 447-2276
loprinzi@gate.net
www.equitablebusiness.com/
loprinzi_guitars

Bill Loveless
15 South Bruce St.
Laurel, MD 20724
(301) 953-9528

Frank Lucchesi
518 Pleasant St.
Holyoke, MA 01040
(413) 532-8819

Mermer Guitars
PO Box 782132
Sebastian, FL 32978
(561) 388-0317
mermer@gate.net
www.gate.net/~mermer

John Mondin
1841 Evergreen
Alton, IL 62002
(314) 895-3403

Brian Moore Custom Guitars
RD 6, Route 22
Brewster, NY 10509
(914) 279-4142

Tom Morici
Ghost Instrument Co.
PO Box 1368
Anaconda, MT 59711
(414) 843-4440

Roy Noble
8140 East Ave. U
Little Rock, CA 93543
(805) 944-5548

José Oribé Guitars
2141 Lakeview Rd.
Vista, CA 92084-7713
(760) 727-2230
Fax (760) 727-2238
oribeg@aol.com
www.oribeguitars.com

William Petersen
6119 Lafayette Ave.
Omaha, NE 68132

Pimentel and Sons
3316 Lafayette Dr. N.E.
Albuquerque, NM 87107
(505) 884-1669
Fax (505) 884-1669
pimentel@rt66.com
www.rt66.com/~pimentel

Tim Quertermous
5702 West 12th
Little Rock, AR 72204
(501) 664-3614

RainSong Guitars
300 Ohukai Rd. #C-214
Kihei, HI 96753
(808) 244-9486
Fax (808) 879-4261
www.rainsong.com

Ron Reed
919 N. 36th St.
Seattle, WA 98103
(206) 634-1662

Jerry Roberts
PO Box 40223
Nashville, TN 37204
Fax (615) 385-3676
www.lamancha.com

Robert Ruck
37676 Hood Canal Dr. N.E.
Hansville, WA 98340
(360) 297-4024

Eric Sahlin
4324 E. 37th Ave.
Spokane, WA 99223
(509) 448-4024

Kirk Sand
1027 N. Coast Hwy.
Laguna Beach, CA 92651
(714) 497-2110

Douglas P. Somervell
2443 Green Cove Rd.
Brasstown, NC 28902
(828) 837-3524

Dake Traphagen
PO Box 724
Bellingham, WA 98227
(360) 671-1017

George Weisel III
Montana Guitarworks
615 Pattee Canyon Dr.
Missoula, MT 59803
(406) 549-2206

Dan Wolf
1652 W. Ethens Glenn
Palatine, IL 60067

Asia

Yoshikane Fukuoka
Fokuoka Musical Instruments
1-23-17 Kichijoji Minami Cho
Musashinoshi, Tokyo 180
Japan
(81) 423-27-3204

Wachira Jinatune
41/14 Moo 8, Charsanitwong 13
R.D. Bangweak
Paseecharden Bangkok 10160
Thailand
(66) 2-410-8841

Kohno Guitars
Distributed by Rokkomann, Inc.
1-16-14 Chihaya
Toshima-Ku, Tokyo 171
Japan
(81) 3-78333-1000
Fax (81) 3-78333-8833

Australia/New Zealand

Ian Kneipp
405 Grey St.
PO Box 696
Glen Innes 2370 NSW
Australia
Phone/fax (61) 6-2667-95674

Ray Mercer
187 Breaker Bay Rd.
Wellington N2
New Zealand
(64) 4-388-2366

Gabriel Ochoteco
Gabriel's Guitar Workshop
158 Barry Parade
Fortitude Valley, Brisbane QLD
Australia 4006

Jim Redgate
46 Penno Parade N.
Belair SA 5052
Australia
(61) 8-8370-3198
redgate@ozemail.com.au
www.ozemail.com.au/~redgate

Greg Smallman
PO Box 510
Glen Innes 2370 NSW
Australia

Canada

Sergei de Jonge
883 Robson St.
Toronto, ON
Canada L1H 4C6
(905) 576-4636

Gregory Furan
38 Stillbrook Ct.
Westhill, ON
Canada M1E 3W7
(416) 284-5622
gfuran@ican.net
www.home.ican.net/~gfuran

Peter Kiss
1017 Gladstone Ave.
Ottawa, ON
Canada K1Y 3G1
(613) 233-1529

Grit Laskin
26 Noble St. #12
Toronto, ON
Canada M6K 2C9
(416) 536-2135

Linda Manzer
65 Metcalfe St., Suite #3
Toronto, ON
Canada M4X 1R9
(416) 927-1539

Wayne O'Connor
Hank to Hendrix Guitars
280 Perry St., Unit 11
Peterborough, ON
Canada K9H 2J4
(705) 740-0965

Mikhail Robert
RR 2, Site 78, Comp. 14
Summerland, BC
Canada V0H 1Z0
(250) 494-8917

Jean Rompré
460 St. Catherine West
Room 914
Montreal, QU
Canada M3B 1A7
(514) 388-1712

Harland Suttis
6065 Cunard St.
Halifax, NS
Canada B3K 1E6
(902) 496-6921
Fax (902) 757-3683

Lloyd Zsiros
367 Knightsbridge Crescent
Ancaster, ON
Canada L9G 3S4
(905) 648-0273

Europe

Paulino Bernabe
Cuchilleros 8
Madrid 12
Spain
(34) 1-3147778
Fax (34) 1-2664430

Guitares Gerard Beuzon
5, rue Abbé Fabre
30250 Sommieres
France
(33) 66-80-30-72
Fax (33) 66-77-73-85

Caprice S.L.
Padre Urbano 31
Valencia 46009
Spain
(34) 9-63668012
Fax (34) 9-63663552

Francois Charle
17 Galerie Vero-Dodat
Paris 75001
France
(33) 14233-3893

Daniele Chiesa
Via Valeria 39
Villa di Serio (BG) 24020
Italy
(39) 0372-34673

Paolo Coriani
via Barchetta 98
Modena 41100
Italy
(39) 0598-27505

Matthias Dammann
Rotthof 104
D-94 152 Neuhaus
Germany
(49) 8507-760

Dominique Field
12, rue Lecuyer
75018 Paris
France
(33) 14252-5406
Fax (33) 14252-8388

Paul Fischer
19 West End
Chipping Norto
Oxfordshire 0X7 5Y
United Kingdom

Ignacio Fleta
4 Calle de Los Angeles
Barcelona 08001
Spain
(34) 9-33171585

Daniel Freiderich
33, rue Sargent Bauchat
Paris 75012
France
(33) 14228-4755

Joaquin Garcia
25 Galica
Malaga 29140
Spain
(34) 9-52621107
Fax (34) 9-52622377

Henner Hagenlocher
Calle Guadarrama N.R. 3
E 18009 76
Granada
Spain

Conde Hermanos
Felipe V2
18013 Madrid
Spain
(34) 9-15470612

Landola Guitars
Rådmansgrand 3 A 12
68620 Jakobstad
Finland

Bernd Martin
Plaza Charca 9
Granada 274193
Spain
(34) 9-58220476

Antonio Marin Montero
Custa del Cardero
Granada 18009
Spain
(34) 9-58228977

Antonio Raya Pardo
Granada, Spain
(34) 9-58228428

José Ramírez
Madrid, Spain
(34) 9-3692212

Ignacio Rozas
Calle Mayor 66
Madrid 28013
Spain
(34) 9-5426921

Otto Vowinkel
Lauriergracht 110
1016 RP Amsterdam
The Netherlands
(31) 20-623-8684
Fax (31) 20-638-7142

Guernot Wagner
Frankfurt, Germany
(49) 6946-4982

Lei Willems
Lenningenhof 47
Eindhoven 5625 NS
The Netherlands
(599) 3140-410051

South/Central America

Sergio Abreu
Avenida Cobacabana 126
Rio de Janeiro 22070
Brasil
(55) 21-521-4818

Luigi Cimafonte
Rua Domingues de Sa No. 413
Icarai
Niteroi R. J. 2420-090
Brasil
(55) 21-711-5313

Abel Garcia Lopez
Guerrero 383, C.P. 60250
Paracho, Michoacan
Mexico
(52) 452-5-02-39

Salons and Shops
Specializing in Classical Guitars

Tom Apodaca Guitars
2260 28th St. #2
Santa Monica, CA 90405
(310) 450-2071

Bridge Classical Guitars
250 8th St.
Brooklyn, NY 11215
(718) 499-0220
www.quikpage.com/b/bclass

R.E. Bruné
800 Greenwood St.
Evanston, IL 60201
(847) 864-7730
Fax (847)864-8022
www.rebrune.com

Classic Guitars International
14622 Ventura Blvd., Suite 108
Sherman Oaks, CA 91403
(818) 788-1463
Fax (818) 788-1407
www.classicguitar.com

Concert Guitars
15634 S.W. 96th Terr.
Miami, FL 33196-3804
(305) 386-4773
Fax (305) 386-5010
www.concertguitars.com

Fine Fretted String Instruments
1645 S. Bascom Ave., 1B
Campbell, CA 95008-0631
(408) 879-9930
Fax (408) 377-2329
www.webnexus.com/users/ffsi

Ruben Flores
PO Box 2746
Seal Beach, CA 90740
(562) 598-9800

The Guitar Salon
45 Grove St.
New York, NY 10014
(212) 675-3236
Fax (212) 367-9767
www.theguitarsalon.com

Guitar Salon International
3100 Donald Douglas Loop N.
Santa Monica, CA 90405
(310) 399-2181
Fax (310) 396-9283
www.guitarsalon.com

Guitar Solo
1401 Clement St.
San Francisco, CA 94118
(415) 386-0395
www.gspguitar.com

Guitarras de España
PO Box 350-071
Brooklyn, NY 11235
(888) 693-6222
www.classguitars.com

Guitars International
Cleveland, OH
(216) 752-7502
Fax (216) 752-7593
www.guitars-int.com

Hand-Picked Guitars
2900 Inkster Rd. #110
Southfield, MI 48034
(248) 799-2299
Fax (248) 799-9966
www.handpickedguitars.com

Maple Street Guitars
3199 Maple Dr. N.E.
Atlanta, GA 30305
(404) 231-5214
Fax (404) 231-5271
www.maplestreetgtrs.com

Jerry Roberts Guitars
PO Box 40223
Nashville, TN 37204
(615) 269-3929
Fax (615) 385-3676
www.lamancha.com

Rosewood Guitar
1406 B N.E. 50th
Seattle, WA 98105
(206) 522-6399
www.halcyon.com/rosewood

Santa Fe Violin and Guitar Works
1412 Llano St.
Santa Fe, NM 87505
(505) 988-4240

Steve's Guitars
1400 Castro
San Francisco, CA 94114
(415) 647-4940
www.successmarketplace.com/
shops/stevesguitars

Taft and Duncan Classical Guitars
4800 Yoakum Blvd.
Houston, TX 77006
(713) 622-1015
Fax (713) 524-6730

The Twelfth Fret
2229 Danforth Ave.
Toronto, ON
Canada M4C 1K4
(416) 694-8026
www.12fret.com

Zavaleta's La Casa de Guitarras
PO Box 37214
Tucson, AZ 85740
(520) 498-1813
Fax (520) 575-6564
www.azstarnet.com/public/
commerce/zavaletas/greene

Organizations

American String Teachers Association (ASTA)
1806 Robert Fulton Dr.
Suite 300
Reston, VA 20191
(703) 476-1316
Fax (703) 476-1317
asta@erols.com
www.astaweb.com
ASTA helps teachers and players develop and refine their skills.

Association of Stringed Instrument Artisans (ASIA)
1394 Stage Rd.
Richmond, VT 05477
(802) 434-5657
luthier@sover.net
A group of guitar and violin makers that meets biannually to share techniques and information and to exhibit their instruments to the public. Publishers of the quarterly *Guitar Maker*.

College Music Society
202 West Spruce St.
Missoula, MT 59802
(406) 721-9616
Fax (406) 721-9419
cms@music.org
www.music.org
A consortium of college, conservatory, university, and independent musicians and scholars interested in composition, ethnomusicology and world music, and music education.

Guild of American Luthiers (GAL)
8222 South Park Ave.
Tacoma, WA 98408
(253) 472-7853
www.luth.org
A group of guitar makers that meets biannually to share techniques and information and to exhibit their instruments to the public. Publishers of the quarterly *American Lutherie*.

Guitar Foundation of America (GFA)
PO Box 1240
Claremont, CA 91711
(909) 624-7730
Fax (909) 624-1151
gunnar@cyberg8t.com
www.cyberg8t.com/gfa
An organization for players and makers of classical guitars that meets annually, organizes a guitar teachers' registry and various newsgroups, and publishes *Soundboard* magazine.

International Guitar Research Archives
California State University
Northridge Music Department
18111 Nordhoff St.
Northridge, CA 91330
igra@csun.edu
www.csun.edu/~igra/
A unique guitar music collection with over 8,000 titles of 19th- and early 20th-century editions, many printed in 19th-century America.

Classical Guitar Education Programs

This list was compiled by the Guitar Foundation of America (GFA), an organization that supports classical guitar makers and players and publishes *Soundboard* magazine (for contact information, see the organizations list at left).

—Simone Solondz

United States

Arizona State University
School of Music
Tempe, AZ 85287-0405
(602) 965-3371
www.asu.edu/cfa/music

Boston Conservatory
8 The Fenway
Boston, MA 02215
(617) 536-6340
Admissions@bostonconservatory.
edu
www.bostonconservatory.edu

California State University at Fullerton
Department of Music
PO Box 34080
Fullerton, CA 92634-9480
(714) 278-3511
www.music.fullerton.edu

California State University at Sacramento
Department of Music
6000 J St.
Sacramento, CA 95819-6015
(916) 278-6543
music@csus.edu or
fenam@gvn.net
www.csus.edu/musc

Cleveland Institute of Music
11021 East Blvd.
Cleveland, OH 44106
(216) 791-5000
cimadmission@po.cwru.edu
www.cim.edu

Eastman School of Music
26 Gibbs St.
Rochester, NY 14604
(716) 274-1000
esmadmit@uhura.cc.rochester.
edu
www.rochester.edu/Eastman

Florida State University
School of Music
Tallahassee, FL 32306-2098
(904) 644-3424
www.music.fsu.edu

Indiana University at Bloomington
School of Music
Bloomington, IN 47405
(812) 855-1582
musicadm@indiana.edu
www.music.indiana.edu

Ithaca College
School of Music
953 Danbury Rd.
Ithaca, NY 14850
(607) 274-3171

The Juilliard School
60 Lincoln Center Plaza
New York, NY 10023-6588
(212) 799-5000
admissions@juilliard.edu
www.juilliard.edu

Loyola University
College of Music
6363 St. Charles
New Orleans, LA 70118
(504) 865-3037
www.loyno.edu/music

Manhattan School of Music
120 Claremont Ave.
New York, NY 10027-4698
(212) 749-2802
www.msmnyc.edu

Mannes College of Music
150 W. 85th St.
New York, NY 10024
(212) 580-0210
www.petersons.com/sites/
405810si.html

New England Conservatory
290 Huntington Ave.
Boston, MA 02115
(617) 585-1101
Fax (617) 585-1115
www.newenglandconservatory.
edu

Oberlin College Conservatory of Music
Oberlin, OH 44074
(419) 775-8200
conad_mail@ocvaxc.cc.oberlin.
edu
www.oberlin.edu/consrv/con.
html

Peabody Conservatory of Music
Johns Hopkins University
1 East Mt. Vernon Pl.
Baltimore, MD 21202
(410) 659-8150
www.peabody.jhu.edu

San Francisco Conservatory of Music
1201 Ortega St.
San Francisco, CA 94122
(415) 564-8086
jog@sfcm.edu
www.sfcm.edu

Southern Methodist University
Division of Music, School
   of the Arts
PO Box 750356
Dallas, TX 75275-0356
(214) 768-2643
www.smu.edu/~music

State College of New York
Department of Music
Buffalo, NY 14260
(716) 636-2765
www.music.buffalo.edu

Stetson University
School of Music
421 N. Woodland Ave.
Unit 8399
DeLand, FL 32720
(904) 822-8975
Fax (904) 822-8948
admissions@stetson.edu
www.stetson.edu/schools/music

Temple University
Esther Boyer College of Music
Philadelphia, PA 19122
(215) 204-8301
music@blue.temple.edu
www.temple.edu/music

University of Akron
School of Music
Akron, OH 44325-1002
(330) 972-7590
www.uakron.edu/faa/schools/
   music.html

University of Arizona
School of Music
Tucson, AZ 85721
(520) 621-1655
inquiry_music@cfa.arizona.edu
arts.music.arizona.edu/music/

**University of California at
Los Angeles (UCLA)**
Department of Music
PO Box 951616
Los Angeles, CA 90095-1616
(310) 825-4761
www.music.ucla.edu

University of Cincinnati
College Conservatory of Music
Cincinnati, OH 45221-0003
(513) 556-3737
Annmarie.Lyons@uc.edu
blues.fd1.uc.edu/www/ccm

**University of Colorado
at Boulder**
College of Music
Campus Box 301
Boulder, CO 80309-0301
(303) 492-6352
Victoria.Ibarra@colorado.edu
www.colorado.edu/music

University of Denver
Lamont School of Music
7111 Montview, Houston FAC
Denver, CO 80220-0195
(303) 871-6400
mbaker@du.edu
www.du.edu/lamont

University of Hartford
The Hartt School
200 Bloomfield Ave.
West Hartford, CT 06117
(860) 768-4454
libaxp.hartford.edu/hartt/
   hartt/www

University of Miami
School of Music
PO Box 248165
Coral Gables, FL 33124-7610
(305) 284-2241
www.music.miami.edu

University of Minnesota
School of Music
2106 Fourth St. S., 200 Ferguson
Minneapolis, MN 55455
(612) 624-4028
mus-adm@maroon.tc.umn.edu
www.music.umn.edu

University of New Mexico
Department of Music
Albuquerque, NM 87131
(505) 277-2126
finearts@unm.edu
www.unm.edu/~finearts/
   music.html

**University of Southern
California**
School of Music
Los Angeles, CA 90089-0851
(213) 740-6935
www.usc.edu/dept/music

University of Texas at Austin
School of Music
25th and East Campus Dr.
Austin, TX 78712-1208
(512) 471-7764
www.utexas.edu/cofa/music

Yale University
School of Music
PO Box 208246
435 College St.
New Haven, CT 06520-8246
(203) 432-1960
music.department@yale.edu
www.yale.edu/yalemus

Canada

McGill University
Faculty of Music
555 Sherbrooke St. W.
Montreal, QU
Canada H3A 1E3
(514) 398-4535
www.music.mcgill.ca

Royal Conservatory of Music
273 Bloor St. W.
Toronto, ON
Canada M5S 1W2
(416) 408-2824
rcm@rcmusic.ca
www.rcmusic.ca

Université de Montréal
Faculty of Music
200, Avenue Vincent-d'Indy
C.P. 6128, Succ. Centreville
Montréal, QU
Canada H3C 3J7
(514) 343-6429
www.musique.umontreal.ca

Université Laval
School of Music
Québec, PQ
Canada G1K 7P4
(418) 656-7061
mus@mus.ulaval.ca
www.ulaval.ca/sg/annuaires/fac/
    mus.html

University of British Columbia
School of Music
6361 Memorial Rd.
Vancouver, BC
Canada V6T 1Z2
(604) 822-3113
www.edziza.arts.ubc.ca

University of Toronto
Faculty of Music
Toronto, ON
Canada M5S 1A1
(416) 978-3750
www.utoronto.ca/music

University of Victoria
School of Music
Box 1700
Victoria, BC
Canada V8W 2Y2
(604) 721-7903
music@uvvm.uvic.ca
kafka.uvic.ca/music

Books

Many of the following books, as well as periodicals, sheet music, and instruments, can be purchased through Guitar Solo, 514 Bryant St., San Francisco, CA 94107; (415) 896-1144; www.gspguitar.com.

William Cumpiano and Jonathan Natelson, *Guitarmaking: Tradition and Techonology,* Chronicle 0-811806-40-5, 1987. Perhaps the most complete guide to building both classical and steel-string guitars. Covers every step, from building your own side-bending jigs to making your own purfling.

Nelson Faria, *The Brazilian Guitar Book,* Sher 1-883217-02-4, 1998 (includes CD). A primer in the seductive rhythms and gentle melodies that have captivated American musicians since the 1950s.

John Morrish, ed., *The Classical Guitar: A Complete History,* Miller Freeman/Hal Leonard 1-871547-46-6, 1997. A large-format volume devoted to the collection of Russell Cleveland and featuring beautifully photographed examples of the work of almost all of the great classical luthiers, from Spanish masters like José Ramírez to modern builders like Greg Smallman and Thomas Humphrey.

Frederick M. Noad, *Solo Guitar Playing, Books 1 and 2,* Frederick Noad/Music Sales 0-8256-1307-8 and 0-0287-1680-9, 1978. With more than a million copies sold, Noad's is the best-selling classical guitar method in the world.

Paco Peña, *Toques Flamencos,* Music Sales 0-8617-5306-2, 1997. Because it is an oral tradition, books on flamenco are rare. This method by venerated artist and teacher Paco Peña teaches the rudiments of flamenco guitar music.

José Romanillos, *Antonio de Torres: His Life and Work,* Bold Strummer 0-9332-2493-1, 1987. A meticulously researched book about the father of the modern classical guitar. Includes photos of the guitars, detailed drawings of the fan bracing Torres pioneered, and a list of all known extant instruments.

Irving Sloane, *Classic Guitar Construction,* Bold Strummer 0-933224-14-1, 1966. The very first how-to book on building guitars. Inspired a generation of luthiers to learn the craft.

Maurice J. Summerfield, *The Classical Guitar: Its Evolution and Its Players Since 1800* (fourth edition), Ashley Mark 1-872639-16, 1998. Detailed biographies of the major classical guitarists, composers, luthiers, scholars, and guitar personalities since 1800.

Harvey Turnbull, *The Guitar from the Renaissance to the Present Day,* Bold Strummer 0-933224-57-5, 1974. A complete history of the classical guitar, including ample information about the instrument's early four- and five-course ancestors.

Periodicals

Acoustic Guitar
String Letter Publishing
PO Box 767
San Anselmo, CA 94979
(415) 485-6946
www.acousticguitar.com

Classical Guitar
Ashley Mark Publishing
1 & 2 Vance Court
Trans Britannia Enterprise Park
Blaydon on Tyne NE21 5NH
England
(44) 191-414-9000
Fax (44) 191-414-9001
www.ashleymark.co.uk/classicalguitar.htm

Guitar Review
Albert Augustine, Ltd.
40 W. 25th St.
New York, NY 10010
(212) 924-4651

Soundboard
Guitar Foundation of America
PO Box 1240
Claremont, CA 91711
www.cyberg8t.com/gfa

About the Author

Acclaimed for her extraordinary lyricism, technique, and versatility, Sharon Isbin has been hailed by critics as "one of our century's best musicians." A Grammy Award nominee, she was first-prize winner of the Toronto Guitar Competition, the first guitarist ever to win the Munich Competition, and winner of the Queen Sofia Competition in Madrid. A frequent guest on Garrison Keillor's *A Prairie Home Companion*, she has been profiled on the nationally televised CBS program *Sunday Morning* and in periodicals from *People* to *Elle*, as well as being featured on the cover of more than 20 magazines.

Isbin tours the world, giving sold-out performances in concert halls including New York's Carnegie Hall and Avery Fisher Hall, Boston's Symphony Hall, Washington D.C.'s Kennedy Center, Toronto's Ford Centre, London's Barbican Centre and Wigmore Hall, Amsterdam's Concertgebouw, Munich's Herkulessaal, and Madrid's Teatro Real. She has appeared in festivals in Hong Kong, Montreux, Strasbourg, Paris, Athens, Istanbul, Budapest, Mexico City, Aspen, and Santa Fe and has been soloist with many of the world's major orchestras, including the London Symphony, Orchestre National de France, National Symphony; Houston, Minnesota, St. Louis, Indianapolis, Milwaukee, Phoenix, Utah, Buffalo, BBC Scottish, Jerusalem, and Tokyo symphonies; as well as the St. Paul, New York, Los Angeles, and Scottish chamber orchestras. She has served as artistic director and featured performer of Carnegie Hall's Guitarstream International Festival, the Ordway Music Theatre's Guitarfest in St. Paul, New York's 92nd Street Y series, and the nationally acclaimed radio series *Guitarjam*.

Isbin's numerous best-selling recordings range from Baroque music to Spanish/Latin, 20th-century, crossover, and jazz fusion, reflecting her remarkable versatility. They have received many awards, including Critic's Choice Recording of the Year in *Gramophone* and *CD Review*, Recording of the Month in *Stereo Review*, and Album of the Year in *Guitar Player*. Joaquín Rodrigo praised her recording of his *Aranjuez* and *Fantasia* concertos as "magnificent." Her all-Latin CD *Journey to the Amazon* (Teldec Classics) with Brazilian percussionist Thiago de Mello and saxophonist Paul Winter received a Grammy Award nomination in 1999 for Best Classical Crossover Album.

Acclaimed for expanding the guitar repertoire with some of the finest new works of the century, Isbin has commissioned and premiered more concertos than any other guitarist, as well as numerous solo and chamber works. *American Landscapes* (EMI/Virgin Classics) with the St. Paul Chamber Orchestra conducted by

Hugh Wolff is the first-ever recording of American guitar concertos and features works written for Isbin by John Corigliano, Joseph Schwantner, and Lukas Foss. (It was launched in the space shuttle Atlantis and presented to Russian cosmonauts during a rendezvous with Mir.) Among the many other composers who have written for Isbin are Christopher Rouse, Tan Dun, Aaron Jay Kernis, Joan Tower, David Diamond, Ned Rorem, John Duarte, and Leo Brouwer.

As a chamber musician, Sharon Isbin has performed with guitar greats Laurindo Almeida, Larry Coryell, Herb Ellis, Stanley Jordan, Michael Hedges, and Carlos Barbosa-Lima, and many others, including Nigel Kennedy, Nadja Salerno-Sonnenberg, Benita Valente, and the Emerson and Cleveland string quartets. She has also collaborated with Antonio Carlos Jobim and shared the stage with luminaries from Aretha Franklin to Muhammad Ali. Born in Minneapolis, she began her studies in Italy at age nine and later studied with Jeffrey Van, Oscar Ghiglia, and Andrés Segovia. After ten years of study with noted keyboardist Rosalyn Tureck, Isbin and Tureck prepared pioneering performance editions of the Bach Lute Suites, which were recorded by Isbin for EMI/Virgin Classics and published by G. Schirmer. She created the Juilliard School Guitar Department in 1989, and she currently serves as director of that department as well as the guitar department at the Aspen Music Festival.

For a complete biography, discography (including sound clips), upcoming concert itinerary, and more, visit Isbin's Web site at www.sharonisbin.com.

Selected Recordings
by Sharon Isbin

You can hear selections from the following CDs and order them directly on Isbin's Web site at www.sharonisbin.com. They are also available at major record stores.

American Landscapes, EMI/Virgin Classics 55083. With the St. Paul Chamber Orchestra and conductor Hugh Wolff. World-premiere recordings of three concertos written for Isbin: *Troubadours* by John Corigliano, *American Landscapes* by Lukas Foss, and *From Afar . . . A Fantasy for Guitar and Orchestra* by Joseph Schwantner.

Appalachian Dreams (title subject to change), Teldec Classics 25736. Fall 1999 release. Includes world-premiere recordings of Duarte's *Appalachian Dreams, Four Songs by Naomi Shemer,* Lauro, Lecuona, and Thiago de Mello. Also includes works by Gismonti, San Sebastian, Granados, and Takemitsu.

Brazil with Love, Concord Picante 4320. With Carlos Barbosa-Lima. Includes works by Jobim, Nazareth, and Pixinguinha.

Journey to the Amazon, Teldec Classics 19899. Grammy award nomination, 1999. With Paul Winter, soprano saxophone, and Thiago de Mello, Brazilian percussion. World-premiere recordings of works by Almeida and de Mello. Also includes music by Savio, Lauro, Barrios, Montaña, Brouwer, and Vianna.

J.S. Bach: Complete Lute Suites, EMI/Virgin Classics 59503.

Love Songs and Lullabies, EMI/Virgin Classics 61480. With Benita Valente, soprano; Thomas Allen, baritone; and Thiago de Mello, percussion.

Nightshade Rounds, EMI/Virgin Classics 45024. World-premiere recordings of Joan Tower's *Clocks* and Bruce MacCombie's *Nightshade Rounds.* Also includes works by Gershwin, Walton, Duarte, and Britten.

Rhapsody in Blue/West Side Story, Concord Concerto 42012. With Carlos Barbosa-Lima.

Road to the Sun/Estrada do Sol: Latin Romances for Guitar, EMI/Virgin Classics 59591. Includes Leo Brouwer's *El Decameron Negro* (written for Isbin) and works by Jobim, Albéniz, Villa-Lobos, Tarrega, Rodrigo, Barrios, Abreu, and Maza.

Rodrigo: Concierto de Aranjuez, EMI/Virgin Classics 59024. With the Lausanne Chamber Orchestra and conductor Lawrence Foster. Includes Rodrigo's *Fantasia para un Gentilhombre* and Vivaldi's Concerto in D.

Wayfaring Stranger, Erato 23419. With mezzo-soprano Susanne Mentzer. World-premiere recordings of Rodrigo's *Aranjuez ma pensée,* as well as American and French folk songs. Includes Schubert lieder and guitar solos by Granados, Tarrega, and Sainz de la Maza.

Sharon Isbin's world-premiere recording of Aaron Kernis' *Double Concerto for Violin, Guitar, and Orchestra* with the St. Paul Chamber Orchestra and conductor Hugh Wolff and violinist Cho-Liang Lin is available on a CD of all Kernis compositions, Argo/Decca 460226. Her world-premiere recording of Joan Tower's *Snowdreams for Flute and Guitar* with flutist Carol Wincenc is available on the all-Tower recording *Black Topaz,* New World 80470.

The Book That Should Have Come With Your Guitar

Better late than never

THE COMPLETE GUIDE
KNOW YOUR INSTRUMENT   PROTECT YOUR INVESTMENT   SOUND YOUR BEST

ITEM # 21330532 $17.95

We predict that some day all new guitars will come equipped with a copy of the *Acoustic Guitar Owner's Manual,* just released by the publishers of *Acoustic Guitar* magazine. After all, you've made a big investment in your guitar. You deserve to know how it works, how to maintain its value, and how to keep it sounding great.

With this definitive and indispensable guide, you'll become a more savvy acoustic guitar owner and repair-shop customer and be able to forego dubious advice from well-meaning friends and anonymous "experts" on the Web. At last, you'll get answers you can trust on these fundamental guitar questions and others:

What's the difference between a dreadnought and a grand concert?

How often should I change strings?

Will installing a pickup affect my vintage guitar's value?

How can I protect my guitar from changes in humidity and temperature?

At your music or book store, or order direct

Call   (800) 637-2852
Fax   (414) 774-3259
On-line **www.acousticguitar.com**

Other Titles from String Letter Publishing

FLATPICKING GUITAR ESSENTIALS

Book and CD
96 pp., $19.95
Item #21699174
ISBN 1-890490-07-5

FINGERSTYLE GUITAR ESSENTIALS

Book and CD
96 pp., $19.95
Item #21699145
ISBN 1-890490-06-7

SWING GUITAR ESSENTIALS

Book and CD
80 pp., $19.95
Item #21699193
ISBN 1-890490-18-0

ROOTS AND BLUES FINGERSTYLE GUITAR

Book and CD
96 pp., $19.95
Item #21699214
ISBN 1-890490-14-8

ALTERNATE TUNINGS GUITAR ESSENTIALS

Book and CD
80 pp., $19.95
Item #21695557
ISBN 1-890490-24-5

ACOUSTIC BLUES GUITAR ESSENTIALS

Book and CD
80 pp., $19.95
Item #21699186
ISBN 1-890490-10-5

ACOUSTIC GUITAR CHORD & HARMONY BASICS

Book and CD
72 pp., $16.95
Item #21695611
ISBN 1-890490-44-X

ACOUSTIC GUITAR SLIDE BASICS

Book and CD
72 pp., $16.95
Item #21695610
ISBN 1-890490-38-5

ACOUSTIC GUITAR LEAD AND MELODY BASICS

Book and CD
64 pp., $14.95
Item #21695492
ISBN 1-890490-19-9

ACOUSTIC GUITAR SOLO FINGER-STYLE BASICS

Book and CD
64 pp., $14.95
Item #21695597
ISBN 1-890490-33-4

ACOUSTIC GUITAR ACCOMPANIMENT BASIC

Book and CD
64 pp., $14.95
Item #21695430
ISBN 1-890490-11-3

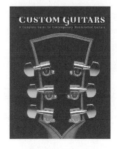

PERFORMING ACOUSTIC MUSIC

104 pp., $14.95
Item #21695512
ISBN 1-890490-22-9

SONGWRITING & THE GUITAR

96 pp., $14.95
Item #21330565
ISBN 1-890490-28-8

ACOUSTIC GUITAR OWNER'S MANUAL

112 pp., $17.95
Item #21330532
ISBN 1-890490-21-0

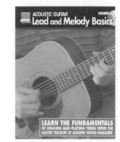

CUSTOM GUITARS

150 pp., $39.95
Item #21330564
ISBN 1-890490-29-6

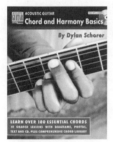

BEST PRIVATE LESSONS

Book and CD
80 pp., $14.95
Item #21695603
ISBN 1-890490-34-2

CLASSICAL GUITAR ANSWER BOOK

84 pp. $14.95
Item #21330443
ISBN 1-890490-08-3

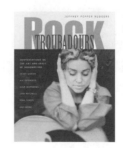

ROCK TROUBADORS

184 pp., $14.95
Item #21330752
ISBN 1-890490-37-7

At your music or book store, or order direct • Call (800) 637-2852 • Fax (414) 774-3259 •
On-line www.acousticguitar.com

On every page of **Acoustic Guitar** Magazine, you'll recognize that same love and devotion you feel for your guitar.

Our goal is to share great guitar music with you, introduce you to the finest guitarists, songwriters, and luthiers of our time, and help you be a smarter owner and buyer of guitars and gear.

You'll also be getting the latest in gear news, artist interviews, practical player advice, songwriting tips, sheet music to play, music reviews, and more, every month.

Acoustic Guitar Magazine wants you to be happy. Let us show you how with THREE FREE issues. So subscribe now without any risk at the low introductory rate of $23.95 for 15 total issues, and enjoy three free issues compliments of *Acoustic Guitar* Magazine. You have our unconditional guarantee: You must be completely satisfied, or your payment will be refunded in full.

Three Free Issues!
Subscribe today
(800) 827-6837
Or, place your order on our Web site!
www.acousticguitar.com

Refer to discount code AGBK01